Revd. A. & Mrs. P. Lindsay
The Rectory
Cambridge Road
Quendon, Saffron Walden
Essex CB11 3XJ
Tel. (01799) 543238

Children Too!

Children Too!

Ideas & Resources for Children's Worship
A Weekly Companion to ASB
Susan Sayers

Worksheets drawn by
Jennifer Carter

Other drawings by
Arthur Baker

Kevin Mayhew

First published in 1995 by
KEVIN MAYHEW LTD
Rattlesden
Bury St Edmunds
Suffolk IP30 0SZ

ISBN 0 86209 647 2
Catalogue No 1500025

Front cover: *The Garden*. An embroidered wool portière
designed by John Henry Dearle (1860-1932).
Reproduced by kind permission of Christie's Images, London.
Cover design by Graham Johnstone

Editor: Alison Sommazzi
Typesetting and Page Creation by Vicky Brown
Printed at Redwood Books, Trowbridge, Wiltshire.

Preface

What are your aims for the children's ministry in your parish? What, as a church, do you most want for the children in your care?

Perhaps it is strange to start an introduction with questions, but they are a kind of 'How do you *do*,' which can lead us immediately into some useful dialogue, sharing our areas of concern and our areas of excitement where things seem to be moving. And that is what *Children Too!* is all about.

It is not a ready-made course so much as a DIY kit, supplied with plenty of openings to meet your own parish needs and spark off your own imaginative ideas. There are some excellent ready-made courses available, but they do not always fit a particular situation, or a particular group of children. They are also quite expensive for churches where the numbers of children are small and/or erratic.

Children Too! is based on the belief that children are as much a part of the church as adults, and that there is great value in sharing the same theme each Sunday, whatever our age. This book follows the weekly themes of the A S B over its two-year cycle, so that the whole church will have that common experience. In order to broaden the scripture base, and to accommodate those parishes whose family worship, church parade or seeker service is non eucharistic, *Children Too!* uses the Morning Prayer lectionary. In each section, the theme for that Sunday is summarized as a 'Thought for the day' and the aim of the children's activities is clearly stated.

Children Too! also includes a series of weekly activity sheets. These may be copied without further permission or charge for non-commercial use, and can be used as they stand, or you can select the material you want. Copy them for the children to take home, use them in church, put them in the magazine or news sheet, distribute them at clubs or Bible study groups or use them in conjunction with your learning programme. There is only one thing they are *not* to be used for, and that is as a lazy substitute for real ministry to the children!

You may find it useful to keep a record of what you actually do each week, as well as build up a store of the resources you use, because this will obviously help to make future activities easier to prepare.

It is my hope that this book will not only stimulate ideas and enable a varied programme of children's work to take place, but most of all it will encourage us, whatever our age, as we make the journey of faith together.

SUSAN SAYERS

Contents

BEFORE CHRISTMAS

9th Sunday before Christmas

YEAR 1

Thought for the day:
This earth is God's earth.

Readings
Psalm 104
Proverbs 8:1, 22-31
Revelation 21:1-7, 22-end

Aim: To help the children sense something of God's creative power.

Play the 'Who made the ice-cream?' game, so they can see that however man-made something appears, if you trace it back, it goes back to God. They like to challenge this claim and can usually think of some pretty unlikely starting points. You can chart their ideas as shown.

This leads on to the obvious question – who made God? Such a deep question is often asked by quite young children and we can delight with them in the mind-blowing answer: nobody made God! God always was, always is and always will be.

Now spend some time examining with magnifying glasses some of the clever designs this amazing alive-for-ever God thinks up. Have a selection of natural objects and pass them round in small groups getting everyone to notice something different about each object. This encourages the children to look really carefully and become more sensitive to the details of design in such

things as we often take for granted. Your selection of objects might include: a piece of evergreen, a stone, a twig of rose-hips, an apple, a cabbage leaf, their own hand. All the objects could be brought into church and displayed, with the title: Our God *is* wise and loving.

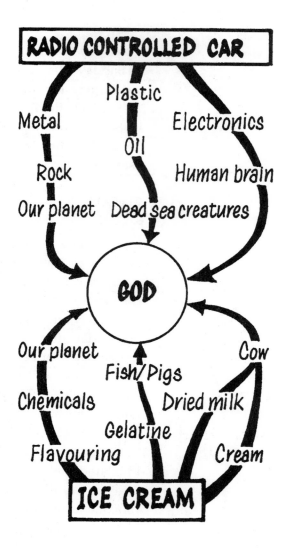

9th Sunday before Christmas

Draw a RED ring round the soft things.

Draw a GREEN ring round the green things.

Draw a BLUE ring round the things with 4 legs.

Draw a YELLOW ring round everything God made.

THE EARTH IS THE LORD'S

Can you unjumble the countries? Now colour in our world

SIARSU
R

PAJNA

HNACI
C

NAIDI
L

IRS NALAC
S L

FIARAC
A

TU ASAARIL
A

9th Sunday before Christmas

YEAR 2

Thought for the day:
This earth is God's earth.

Readings
Psalm 104
Job 38:1-21; 42:1-6
Acts 14:8-17

Aim: To help the children realise that for God nothing is impossible.

Show and talk about something you have managed to make, but which you needed a bit of help with. Let the children share about something they have made and are really proud of. Talk together about how nice it is when you get to a really tricky bit if someone is there to sort you out.

In the centre of the circle, have a few children to help you tell the story by acting it out. Now narrate today's Acts reading, from the healing of the lame man through to the people thinking Paul and Barnabas had done the healing themselves. Stop and ask the children what they think – if it wasn't them, then who had made the man better?

Can God really do something as amazing as that?

Thank the volunteer actors and lay out in the circle lots of pictures of our beautiful creation – from stars and planets to tiny insects. Put on some music while you and the children wander round very quietly, thanking God for each thing he has made.

Now we can see that God is so great that anything is possible for him, no matter how difficult it may seem for us.

GOD is the one who made

20,8,5   19,11,25

20,8,5
5,1,18,20,8

1,14,4   1,12,12   20,8,1,20
9,19   9,14,   20,8,5,13

20,8,5
19,5,1

Colour these
creatures and draw
some of your own:

A	B	C	D	E	F	G	H	I	J	K	L	M	N	O	P	Q	R	S	T	U	V	W	X	Y	Z
1	2	3	4	5	6	7	8	9	10	11	12	13	14	15	16	17	18	19	20	21	22	23	24	25	26

8th Sunday before Christmas

YEAR 1

Thought for the day:
Sin destroys us; God can save us.

Readings
Psalm 25
Isaiah 44:6-22
1 Corinthians 10:1-13 (or 24)

Aim: To help the children to understand that in Christ they can fight against evil.

Give each child two matching sheets of paper. They should create one picture gloomy and nasty, the other light and colourful, using paints, felts or collage. Draw lines the width of a ruler down one picture, place the other one behind it and cut both pictures into matching strips. On another sheet of paper or thin card, stick the strips alternately. Fold the completed sheet like a fan, keeping to the edges of the strips of pictures. When this is viewed from one side, you can only see the evil and darkness. But when you turn it a bit, you can see it change into brightness and joy.

Explain that sometimes we can feel like the dark picture, with no power to avoid being unkind/jealous/angry etc. That's the time to remember to ask God to give us his power to put things right, and he will transform the way we are looking and help us sort things out.

8th Sunday before Christmas

Sin :(destroys us...

Colour in horrible colours

God can Save us

:) ~Colour in your favourite colours

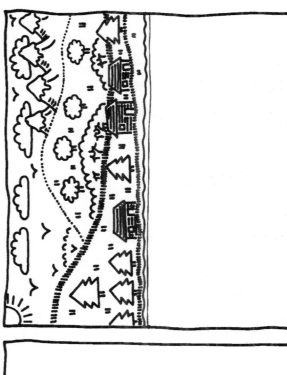

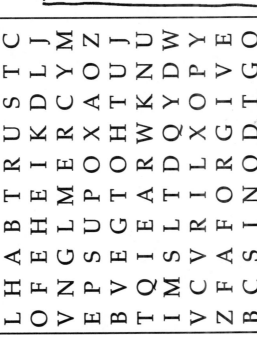

Draw the reflections and colour the pictures.

REFLECT GOD'S LOVE
REFLECT GOD'S LOVE

```
L H A B T R U S T C
O F E H E I K D L J
V N G L M E R C Y M
E P S U P O X A O Z
B V E G T O H T U J
T Q I E A R W K N U
I M S L T D Q Y D W
V C V R I L X O P Y
Z F A F O R G I V E
B C S I N O D T G O
```

EVIL   TEMPTATION
SIN   MERCY
LOVE   FORGIVE
TRUST   GOD
HELP   YOU

8th Sunday before Christmas

YEAR 2

Thought for the day:
Sin destroys us; God can save us.

Readings
Psalm 25
Jeremiah 17:5-14
Romans 5:12-end

Aim: To help the children see that we can trust God to save us.

Play a trust game first. One idea is for the children to get into pairs, with one of the pair blindfolded. The blindfolded person is then led round an obstacle course.

Afterwards discuss with the children how they needed to trust their partner for the game, otherwise they would have been in danger of getting hurt. Talk about times they have felt let down by people, and recognise that because we are weak as humans, we can't expect humans never to let us down. But we can certainly trust God never to let us down, however, difficult or frightening life gets.

Show the children a length of cotton contrasted with a length of really strong rope. They can try pulling on each. God is like the strong rope, and whenever they feel frightened, or lonely, or tempted to do something cruel, they can hang on tightly to the strong rope of God's love and it will never let them down.

8th Sunday before Christmas

TRUST IN GOD WHO IS GOOD

Draw the tree here.

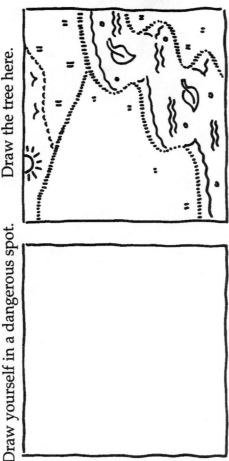

Draw yourself in a dangerous spot.

Blessed is the one who ▓▓▓ in the ☐. He ◠ be like a ✿ planted by the ⬡. It does not ⬡ when ◈ comes, its ◗ are always ▭.

fear

(green

Lord

will

trust

heat

water

tree

leaves

Draw what they really look like

Put a ring round the mirror you would trust to reflect you best

7th Sunday
before Christmas

YEAR 1

Thought for the day:
God chooses Abraham;
Abraham responds in faith.

Readings
Psalms 32, 36
Genesis 18:1-9
Romans 9:1-13

Aim: To learn about choosing and responding.

Tell the children today's story about Abraham receiving his guests and being told that although he and his wife are old, they are going to have a son. Point out how God had chosen Abraham for something which must have seemed pretty impossible, but his trust in God made it possible. Then follow a recipe together so that by following the instructions you end up with something nice to eat.

GOD CHOSE ABRAHAM

Did Abraham Say YES or No ? to God

What did he choose Abraham for?

KEY:

Put a ring round the things you would choose to take on holiday.
We choose things we trust to be useful.

Colour the dotted bits:

7th Sunday before Christmas

YEAR 2

Thought for the day:
God chooses Abraham;
Abraham responds in faith.

Readings
Psalms 32, 36
Isaiah 55
Galatians 3:1-14

Aim: Helping children to understand that we don't earn God's love, as it's freely given.

Have a nice box of chocolates on display as a prize. For the group to win it everyone must answer one question correctly. With the atmosphere of a quiz show, give each person a question they can definitely answer until you get to the last person. (Make sure this is someone fairly self confident to avoid anyone being upset.) Ask this person a question which is impossible to answer, rather than just hard. For instance: Who is driving past West Leigh school at the moment?

Weather all the protests at the unfairness and impossibility of the question and savour the disappointment a little. Then explain that it's obvious they can't win the chocolates even though they all tried very hard, and that's the bad news. That's true with God's love as well – there's nothing we can do to earn it.

But there's good news too. Jesus told us that God loves us all the time already. He offers us his love for free. (As you say this, take the wrapping off the chocolates ready to hand them round.) What we have to do is choose whether to say 'Yes please' or 'No thank you'. Go round the group saying to each one, 'Will you enjoy one of my chocolates?' If they say 'Yes please' they can have one and you can all enjoy them together.

In a time of prayer, remind them that God offers each of us his love to make our lives full of love and peace and joy. All we have to do is to say to him 'Yes please'.

GOD'S LOVE COMES FREE OF CHARGE!

Draw some things you have had as presents and write underneath who gave them to you.

Most things cost money.
Some things are expensive.
God gives us his love.
It cost him his life.

Which of these things must you do to win God's love?

50p

£1

35p

10p

How much is the pen?

How much is the drink?

Does the pen cost the most?

Is the balloon cheap?

Can you buy 3 things for a £1?

What does it cost to buy all the things?

Is anything free?

6th Sunday
before Christmas

YEAR 1

*Thought for the day:
God is a rescuer and redeemer
of his people.*

Readings
Psalm 66
Deut. 18:15-end
Acts 3

Aim: To help the children see that Jesus fulfils the prophets.

Write the names of the prophets on a large chart as follows:

Isaiah, Jeremiah, Ezekiel Hosea, Joel, Amos, Obadiah, Micah, Nahum, Habakkuk, Zephaniah, Haggai, Zechariah, Malachi.

Also display a large copy of the grid illustrated.

Don't mention the 'prophets' at this stage but say these are the names of men in the Old Testament. Then ask the children to answer the following questions so that the grid can be filled in:

1   Which name contains the letter 'p'?
2   Which name has 'r' as its third letter?
3   Which name ends in 'a'?
4   Which name contains the letters of 'human'?
5   Which name contains a 'z' and 'k'?
6   Which name has two 'i's and two 'a's?
7   Which name begins with 'A'?
8   Which name contains two 'g's?
9   Which four letter name begins with 'J'?
10 Which name begins with 'O'?

The vertical row below the arrow should read PROPHETS OF GOD.

Explain who the prophets were and what they did.

Then look at some of these things the prophets said (have them written out clearly on pieces of card) and see if the children can work out how the prophecies came true in Jesus. You could use such verses as Micah 5:2; Isaiah 7:14; 9:6; 11:1, 2; 53:3, 4; 61:1,2; Zechariah 9:9. Have a selection of books and pictures for the children to search through and when the pictures have been matched up with the prophecies, display them all on the floor.

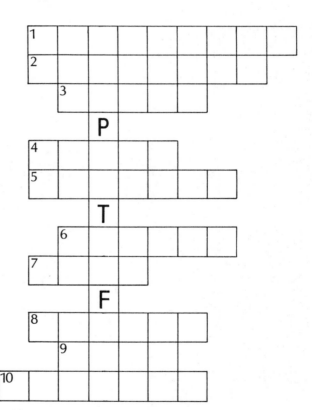

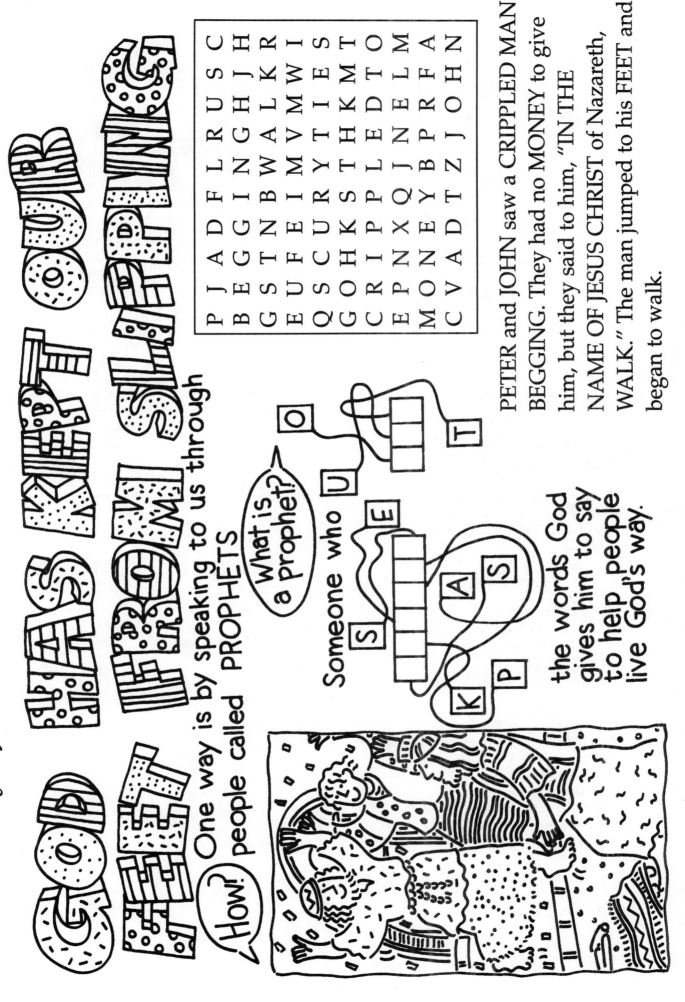

6th Sunday before Christmas

GOD HAS KEPT OUR FEET FROM SLIPPING

One way is by speaking to us through people called PROPHETS

What is a Prophet?

Someone who _ _ _ _ _ _ _ _ the words God gives him to say to help people live God's way.

S O U T K P A E S

P	J	A	D	F	L	R	U	S	C
B	E	G	G	I	N	G	H	J	H
G	S	T	N	B	W	A	L	K	R
E	U	F	E	I	M	V	M	W	I
Q	S	C	U	R	Y	T	I	E	S
G	O	H	K	S	T	H	K	M	T
C	R	I	P	P	L	E	D	T	O
E	P	N	X	Q	J	N	E	L	M
M	O	N	E	Y	B	P	R	F	A
C	V	A	D	T	Z	J	O	H	N

PETER and JOHN saw a CRIPPLED MAN BEGGING. They had no MONEY to give him, but they said to him, "IN THE NAME OF JESUS CHRIST of Nazareth, WALK." The man jumped to his FEET and began to walk.

6th Sunday before Christmas

YEAR 2

Thought for the day:
God is a rescuer and redeemer
of his people.

Readings
Psalm 66
Exodus 1:8-14, 22-2:10
Hebrews 3

Aim: To help the children see the difference between looking at God's creation and looking through it to God.

Have plenty of coloured cellophane toffee wrappers. (You may need to eat some toffees first.) Ask everyone to look at their wrapper carefully and tell one another what they can see on it. There may be the odd sticky patches, wrinkly bits, creases, slits or specks of dust.

Now try looking through the wrappers and notice how everything changes colour. If there is enough time, let them swap the wrappers around to see all the different colours.

Tell the story of Moses with the help of some visual aids and willing actors, drawing the story from the children if they are already familiar with it. Explain how we can look at Moses and learn a lot from him (just as we looked straight at our wrappers) but we can also find that, as Moses was God's friend, looking at his life helps us to see God in a new way (as we saw everything differently when we looked through our wrappers).

Make this model using a toffee wrapper and card.

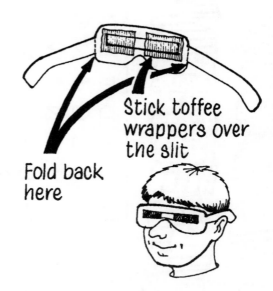

Stick toffee wrappers over the slit

Fold back here

6th Sunday before Christmas

BABY MOSES IS HIDDEN IN A FLOATING BASKET

Can you find a FISH, a FROG, a SNAIL and an ANT in the picture?

GOD TO THE RESCUE!

God uses us to help sort things out. Match the people to the problems.

set us free from sin

Moses being saved from being killed

Show God's love at home by ....

Moses

You

JESUS

Moses mother

Led the people out of slavery.

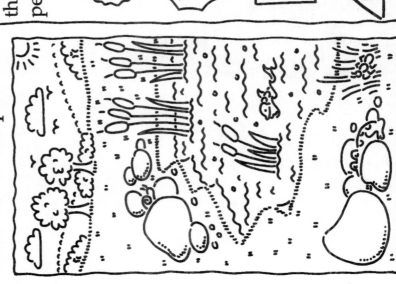

Now you can colour it in.

5th Sunday before Christmas

YEAR 1

Thought for the day:
God preserves a remnant,
whatever the surrounding evil.

Readings
Psalm 147
Genesis 18:20-end
Mark 13:14-end

Aim: Sorting out and rescuing the faithful.

Bring along with you a pile of old greetings cards. Start by asking the children to sort these into ones which can be used for messages and those which can't be as they have writing on the back of the picture. Make a pile of the usable ones and put the others ready for recycling.

Tell the children the story from Exodus, bringing out the fact that although the city was so wicked, God still gathered Lot's family and saved them before the city was destroyed. He loves to rescue us from doing unkind, unloving things. When we turn a light on in a dark room the darkness can't survive. In the light of God's love evil can't survive.

Use the good cards to write this message: 'Jesus to the rescue!'.

EVIL WON'T SURVIVE—BUT GOOD WILL.

Block out all the evil bits and see what's left

Saving what's good

What could you save from these things?

The city of ▢▢▢▢ was very ▢▢▢. begged God to save it, if a few good ▢▢▢▢ could be ▢▢▢▢▢ in it. But there were ▢▢ even 10 good people in Sodom so it was destroyed.

ABRAHAM NOT FOUND PEOPLE SODOM EVIL

5th Sunday before Christmas

YEAR 2

Thought for the day:
God preserves a remnant, whatever the surrounding evil.

Readings
Psalm 147
Genesis 6:5-end
1 Peter 3:8-end

Aim: To encourage the children to stick to what is right.

If you can bear the embarrassment, bring along a few things you have tried to make which have turned out badly, or something you loved which has got broken.

Begin by playing the 'sleeping lions' game, where everyone has to lie completely still, however much the others tempt them to move. Talk together about how difficult it is to keep lying still when you are being encouraged to move, and how difficult it is to keep on doing what you know is right when everyone around is persuading you not to bother. (e.g. not wanting to join in a 'be nasty to so-and-so' game; wanting to walk straight home from school when others want you to use a short-cut you've been told not to use.)

Now reveal to the children your disaster, to tell them about it. If any of them want to, they can share disasters they have had. Talk about how disappointed we feel when we try really hard to make something well and it turns out badly. Or how miserable it is when something we have made and are fond of gets broken.

That's how God felt and feels when he sees the people he has made so carefully all getting at one another and spoiling things. With the aid of pictures of models, get the children to help you tell the story of God rescuing Noah and the animals from the wicked world.

Help the children make this working model to remind them: DON'T GET SUCKED IN – STICK TO WHAT'S RIGHT.

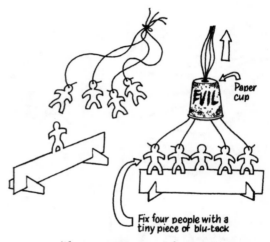

Fix four people with a tiny piece of blu-tack

When you pull the strings, four people get tempted into evil, one stays where s/he is.

5th Sunday before Christmas

GOD KEEPS NOAH SAFE

Draw the other animals so there are 2 of each sort.

It may be tough, but...

even when people try to put you off.

Draw in the water, the rain, the clouds and the lightning.

ADVENT

1st Sunday in Advent

YEAR 1

Thought for the day:
Keep alert, because much is demanded
of those to whom much is entrusted.

Readings
Psalm 18:1-32
Isaiah 1:1-20
Luke 12:35-48

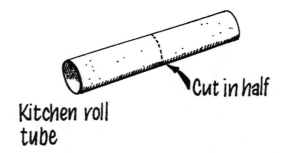

Kitchen roll tube

Cut in half

Tape rolls together and tape string on to sides

Aim: To help the children recognise that sin creeps up on us if we aren't watchful.

Give the children large labels to wear round their necks, or headbands which have on them such things as: being greedy, being mean, being unkind, being thoughtless, being rude, being lazy etc.

Play the Mr. Wolf game with a difference, with all the evil creeping upon Mr. Wolf while he isn't looking. Mr. Wolf can only stop the evil getting at him by catching sight of someone moving. Point out that the more watchful he is, the less chance there is of them getting him. Now read the passage from Luke 12 to them, and help them make a pair of cardboard binoculars to remind themselves to keep watchful.

KEEP WATCHFUL

WATCH OUT!

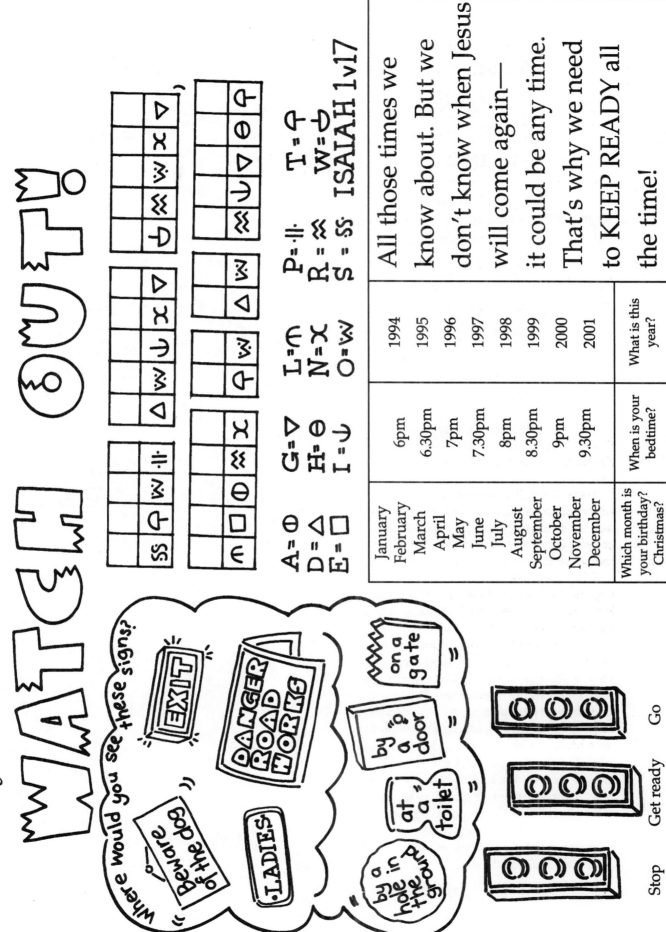

A = Θ   G = ▽   L = ⋒   P = ∦   T = Ϙ
D = △   H = θ   N = ✕   R = ⋈   W = ⊌
E = □   I = ⌄   O = ⊍   S = §§

ISAIAH 1 v 17

All those times we
know about. But we
don't know when Jesus
will come again—
it could be any time.
That's why we need
to KEEP READY all
the time!

Which month is your birthday? Christmas?	When is your bedtime?	What is this year?
January		1994
February		1995
March	6pm	1996
April	6.30pm	1997
May	7pm	1998
June	7.30pm	1999
July	8pm	2000
August	8.30pm	2001
September	9pm	
October	9.30pm	
November		
December		

Where would you see these signs?

EXIT

DANGER ROAD WORKS

Beware of the dog

LADIES

on a gate

by a door

at a toilet

by a hole in the ground

Stop   Get ready   Go

1st Sunday in Advent

YEAR 2

Thought for the day:
Keep alert, because much is demanded
of those to whom much is entrusted.

Readings
Psalm 18:1-32
Isaiah 2:10-end
Matthew 24:1-28

Aim: To explore getting ready and being ready.

Have some different types of work clothing, such as a judo suit, Brownie gear, school uniform, football strip, overall etc. Also have a house plant and watering can and/or a small pet.

As you get different children to dress up, talk about how we have to get prepared to do things, and we enjoy it while we're feeling keen. Then we might start getting fed up with it. (Get them to undress back into ordinary clothes again.) Even if we're actually still going along, we're rather lazy about it now.

Talk about the importance in our Christian life not only of getting ready but of keeping ready. Show the children the house plant and/or small pet – the getting ready is exciting, but we also have to keep on with the feeding and watering and so on, or the plants and pets would die. If we want our faith to stay alive, we've got to look after that as well, feeding it with praying and reading the bible. This would be a good opportunity to have a few different bible reading schemes on show to look at, and on sale for parents afterwards.

CHRIST will come again

WORD SEARCH

```
J  !  A  F  P  T  V  B
E  B  O  O  ?  E  R  A
S  D  M  R  N  Q  U  C
U  L  C  K  I  W  Y  K
S  ?  R  E  A  D  Y  !
Y  E  M  J  S  R  X  A
F  O  G  !  H  I  M  ?
C  H  U  Z  W  I  L  L
```

JESUS
WILL
COME
BACK!
ARE
YOU
READY
FOR
HIM?

Did you know that one day
(we don't know which day)
Jesus will come back again,
and on that day everyone in
the whole world will see him.

Colour the Picture very carefully

Draw what happens next

Jesus told us there would
be ☐☐ in the ☐☐
and ☐☐☐, there would
be ☐☐ and ☐☐☐☐☐☐☐
before he comes again.

wars
sun
moon
earthquakes
signs

What does this sign mean?

2nd Sunday
in Advent

YEAR 1

Thought for the day:
The Word of God has been gradually
unfolded all through the
Old Testament, throughout
the New Testament and ever since.

Readings
Psalm 119:137-152
1 Kings 22:1-28
Romans 10:5-17

Aim: To explore the story in 1 Kings 22.

Tell the story with the children's help. They will be acting it out. Use dressing up clothes and appropriate props to make it realistic. Emphasise the importance of finding out God's will before we rush ahead and do things that we want to. Then make these badges to wear.

LOOKING AT THE BIBLE

One of the ways we can find out what God is like is to read the Bible. The ⊞ Testament looks forward to the coming of Jesus. The ⊞ Testament is about Jesus and his followers.

The Bible has lots of books in it. Here are some of them~ cross out every second letter to find them: AMCSTUSY

LJUBKMEX

JHOMHANS

GBEJNOERSTILSNPRSBALLOMTSJ

ITSWAYIMANHT

Find Psalm 119 verse 105 and write the words here:

Your ____ is
a ~~~~
to ~ ~~~~
and a ~~~~
to ~ ~~

IN

WORD   GOD

AND   THE

THE   HEAR

WE   OF

READ

BIBLE   CAN

The BIBLE

Design a cover for this bible is

2nd Sunday in Advent

Check how the bible reading is going and help them make this pair of ears to remind themselves to listen to what God is saying.

YEAR 2

Thought for the day:
The Word of God has been gradually
unfolded all through the
Old Testament, throughout
the New Testament and ever since.

Readings
Psalm 119:137-152
Jeremiah 36:9-end (or 26)
Matthew 25:14-30

Aim: To teach the children to listen.

First play this listening game. Tell the story from Jeremiah giving each person a part. Whenever they hear themselves mentioned, they stand up, turn around and sit down. At the mention of the fire, everyone moves. Afterwards point out how they had all needed to listen to do that so well. Who in the story didn't want to hear what God has to say? Did he succeed in destroying God's word when he burnt the scrolls? (For a little while, but not for long.) Who was good at listening to God?

Now try listening to hear a pin drop, first with your ears blocked and then normally. Try looking at something with your eyes closed and then with them open. Try feeling something with thick gloves on and then without. That's how we are, sometimes; God communicates with us in lots of ways, but if we want to notice, we'll have to listen carefully.

THROUGH THE BIBLE GOD SPEAKS TO US.

Write the names in the right shapes

Gospels

Micah

(Matthew)

Mark

ISAIAH

John

Prophets

Luke

EZEKIEL

Jeremiah

The Bible was written on SCROLLS like this. You roll up the book instead of turning the pages.

Find Psalm 119 verse 89 and write it in here:

....

....

....

Colour in:
Bible places = BLUE
Bible people = RED
Bible kings = GREEN

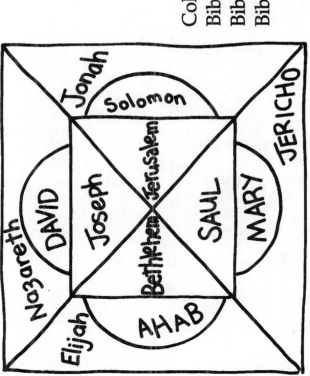

Jonah

Solomon

Nazareth

DAVID

Joseph

Bethlehem Jerusalem

SAUL

MARY

JERICHO

Elijah

AHAB

3rd Sunday
in Advent

YEAR 1

Thought for the day:
Through his messengers God prepares
the way for salvation.

Readings
Psalm 80
Amos 7
Luke 1:1-25

Aim: To introduce the children to John the Baptist.

Begin by enlisting everyone's help in getting the place ready for painting. When this is done, point out how we needed to change things in the room, putting them in new places, so that the room was ready. Today we are going to look at someone who helped people prepare their lives so they would be ready to meet Jesus.

Now tell the story of Zechariah and Elizabeth, adding that when the baby grew up he did just what the angel had said – he helped people get ready for Jesus. Ask them to think of one thing in their lives which they know is not right – telling lies/not going to bed when they're told/being rude/not sharing/being a bad loser etc. and suggest they try and tackle that one thing through Advent.

Use the paints to make a large picture of John the Baptist baptising people in the Jordan. Call it: GETTING READY FOR JESUS.

JOHN GETS THE PEOPLE READY

Which one is getting ready for what?

JOHN THE BAPTIST
HELPED PEOPLE GET READY

"How do you do that?"

"See if you can help..."

"How?"

"By straightening their lives out."

Meg thinks she is totally wonderful...

Chris is very greedy

Bill steals things

Pat and Sue are always fighting

How can these people get ready?

```
B C L H R T Q
A K J A G H N
P E O P L E S
T D H B F T O
I I N J E M V
S E P G U W X
T T R E A D Y
H E L P E D Z
```

Colour in the picture

3rd Sunday in Advent

YEAR 2

Thought for the day:
Through his messengers God prepares
the way for salvation.

Readings
Psalm 80
1 Kings 18:17-39
Luke 3:1-20

Aim: To help the children get their lives ready for Christmas.

You will need a height chart, pieces of card, templates of crosses, coloured pens and scissors.

Tell them the story of John the Baptist helping everyone get ready for Jesus by making sure their lives were in line with the way God wanted them to live. How do they think God does want us to live? (Some of the answers may be very interesting!) Write up the main ideas inside the shape of a cross. We know God wants us to be like this because Jesus was like this, even though it brought him pain and suffering.

Show the children the height chart that we can check our height against. (Some children can demonstrate).

As Christians we have to check the way we are living against God's standard of LOVE. Help the children make these life-checkers:

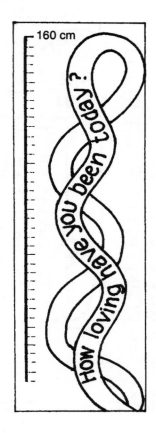

PREPARE THE WAY OF THE LORD

John the Baptist prepared people for Jesus.
Colour this road as you like:

Saying sorry=BLUE

forgiving=GREEN

Stop cheating=RED

stop swearing=YELLOW

Workmen prepare a new road.
Colour the picture carefully:

You can't tell from the outside what someone is like, but God knows us inside and out. Which of these people

is **mean** ?   Who is **kind** ?   Who is **selfish** ?

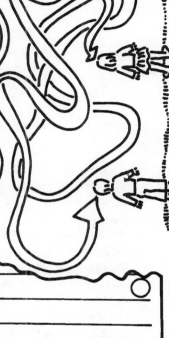

Today I will be kind by...

Draw yourself in two kind, thoughtful things.

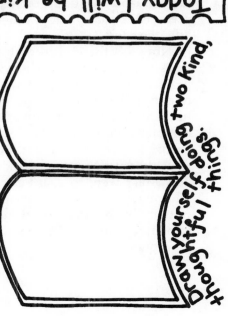

4th Sunday in Advent

YEAR 1

Thought for the day:
After years of waiting, the Lord is very near.

Readings
Psalm 40
1 Samuel 1:1-20
Luke 1:39-55

Aim: To meet some people who worked with God by trusting him.

Beforehand prepare card pictures of Zechariah, Elizabeth, Joseph and Mary; Elizabeth and Mary are both looking very happy. Also make a signpost which says 'To Nazareth', and Elizabeth's house. Put down the story mat, or green and blue sheets/carpet tiles.

Get the children to tell the story of Gabriel visiting Mary to tell her that she would have a son who would save his people. (This is something most will be familiar with already.) Point out how Mary said she was happy for it all to happen God's way, and how Joseph was prepared to marry her and help her look after the baby.

Now tell the children about Mary's cousin, Elizabeth; the way she had prayed for a child and was now six months pregnant with John, and how her husband had been told by an angel how his son would prepare the way for Jesus.

Using the story mat and figures, with the children adding trees and paths, tell how Mary went to visit her cousin, and what happened when they met. (Those with baby brothers and sisters may remember how babies move around in the womb.)

Help the children make these cards to remind them to say 'Yes' to God.

Front

 Push in split pin to form a handle not at the front but at the BACK of the door.

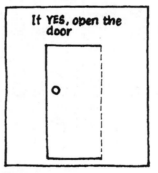

Back

THE ANGEL VISITS MARY

The angel told Mary:-

Jesus · To · Name · Going · Are · A · His · You · Have · Will · Be · Baby

Colour the picture carefully.

What was the name of the angel?

Mary was 🙂 ☹️ . She said NO / YES

4th Sunday in Advent

YEAR 2

Thought for the day:
After years of waiting, the Lord is very near.

Readings
Psalm 40
Jeremiah 33:10-16
Revelation 22:6-end

Aim: To help the children understand that we are both looking backwards and forwards at Christmas.

Talk about looking back to times we have enjoyed – you could show some holiday snaps to give them the idea. Ask them to think back to this year's summer holiday and then forward to the things they want to do again next year.

At Christmas we are looking back to the time when Jesus came to live among us as a human person. We're also looking forward to the time he has promised to come back again. (To many children this comes as a great surprise and they have lots of questions about it. Answer them without surmising anything, recognising that even Jesus himself didn't know when it would be, but we do know it will happen, whether we are alive or dead at the time.)

Help them make this model to remember that we are preparing for both events.

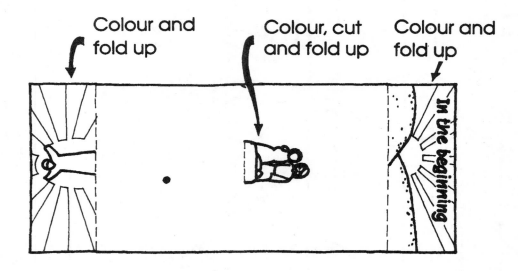

Colour and fold up   Colour, cut and fold up   Colour and fold up

In the beginning

Move the person
to look back at the crib and
forward to the second coming

Colour yourself,
fold flap and fix
dot to dot with split pin

MARY SAID 'YES'

Who is in your family tree?

Draw them or write their names in here:

Dad

Mum

Your Grandads and Nans

We were trapped in our SIN.

God had a RESCUE plan.
He would be born as a [ ][ ][ ][ ]Y.

He would need a good, loving mother.
Who did God choose?

Q. Why is Jesus sometimes called the 'Son of David'?
A. Because Joseph (Mary's husband) was part of King David's family tree

king
David's
family
tree
of
part
was
Joseph
START

Help the rescue team to reach the trapped man.

CHRISTMASTIDE

Christmas Day

YEARS 1 AND 2

Thought for the day:
Jesus Christ is God's good news in
language humankind can understand.

Readings
Psalm 19
Isaiah 35
John 3:16-21

Christmas morning is very much a time for all God's children to worship together, so I have not included any separate ideas for the children alone. They will be included in the following all-age activity.

Aim: To show that the incarnation means that God is with us in person.

You will need some kind of transformer toy, a road map book of your country and a model car (preferably a sit-in one). Explain that you have brought along some Christmas presents to talk about.

First show the transformer and ask its owner to show how it changes from one thing into another. Perhaps some people expected the familiar 'Christmassy' readings of Mary and Joseph, the manger, and angels and the shepherds this morning. What we actually heard was the promise of impossible transformation taking place in our world due to God's complete love for us. Like this transformer, God coming in person into our lives means that he can change us from being selfish into being loving; he can change us from being trapped by guilt and fear into being free to live abundantly and enjoy life to the full.

Now show the road map. Anyone travelling over the Christmas holiday will really appreciate having one of these, because whenever you get to a confusing junction which suddenly stops sign-posting the place you are trying to get to you can look here and see the whole picture, rather than just the muddy spray and tarmac around you. Now that God is with us in person our lives can be guided, and the best route taken.

As it's Christmas day we'll play a party game now. It's a sort of 'Give us a clue" and it will help us remember what Christmas really celebrates. One word, first syllable: IN (ask someone to climb into the pedal car). Second syllable: CAR (ask the person in the car to drive it around). Third and fourth syllable: NATION (get the road map book and point to the name of the country on the front, or show the complete map of the area in the front of the book). Whole word, which means the great news that God is with us in person: INCARNATION. (In extrovert gatherings everyone can shout it. In more demure congregations, everyone can tell it to someone else.)

Christmas Day

Colour this picture of the shepherds on the hills above Bethlehem. WHAT HAPPENED NEXT?

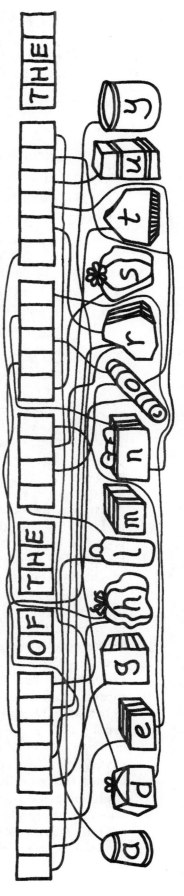

1st Sunday
after Christmas

YEAR 1

Thought for the day:
Laying his glory and majesty aside,
God is content to enter human life as
a vulnerable baby.

Readings
Psalm 132
Isaiah 40:18-end
Colossians 1:1-20

Aim: To help the children appreciate the greatness and majesty of God.

You will need a number of wildlife magazines, calendars and seed catalogues for cutting up, scissors, glue, pens and a large sheet of card. Also some reference books with good pictures of the universe and our planet viewed from space. A few percussion instruments may be used too.

First look at the reference books together, helping the children imagine the size and beauty of the universe God has made. Then make a working model of the solar system using one child to be the sun and nine others of varying sizes to be the planets. These children move slowly round the sun in their orbits while any remaining children play some quiet 'space music'. Or everyone can sing a worship song such as 'All that I am' (Spring Harvest – *Kid's Praise 1992*).

Then help the children to make a collage picture of the beauty of our created universe, including on it written truths about God, such as 'Our God loves what he has made'; 'Heaven and earth are full of his glory'.

1st Sunday after Christmas

JESUS IS BORN

Colour this picture carefully. As you do it, thank God for coming into our world.

ANGEL
MANGER
MARY
JOSEPH
DONKEY
STAR
INN
STABLE

```
M A H F N U R V
A J W M E A O B
R C O B T L T S
Y G X S Q L K T
D O N K E Y P A
Q I I G D P A B
Y R N S Z J H L
M A N G E R C E
```

What town was Jesus born in?

1st Sunday after Christmas

YEAR 2

Thought for the day:
Laying his glory and majesty aside,
God is content to enter human life as
a vulnerable baby.

Readings
Psalm 132
Haggai 2:1-9
1 Peter 2:1-10 or Luke 2:41-end

Aim: To help the children see that God works in us to put things right where they have gone wrong.

You will need a number of cartons and boxes and other interesting junk to build with, plenty of sticky tape and parcel tape, staples and pens.

First remind the children of how smart King Solomon's temple had been. Get them to make the temple with their bodies, bit by bit, like this:

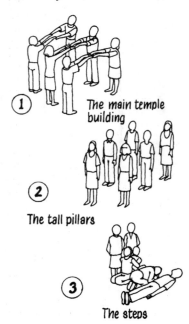

① The main temple building

② The tall pillars

③ The steps

Now explain how after many years of being unfaithful to God, the temple was attacked and reduced to rubble. (Everyone falls down.) Many people were taken off to Babylon.

Then, after 70 years, the people were allowed to return, and all they found was their beautiful temple in ruins. As the children lie there, read them Haggai's words, and then let them slowly rebuild themselves. Tell them how God can rebuild us whenever we fall down through doing or thinking or saying what is unloving or evil, and help them use some useless junk to build into a superb structure.

GOD IS WITH US.

God let some shepherds share the secret. Most people thought shepherds were unclean but God loved them. Do you know what the angels sang to them?

| 3 | 6 | 8 | 9 | 12 | | 11 | 8 | | 3 | 8 | 1 |

| 11 | 4 | 2 | | 4 | 5 | 3 | 4 | 2 | 10 | 11 |

| 5 | 7 |

D	E	G	H	I	L	N	O	R	S	T	Y
1	2	3	4	5	6	7	8	9	10	11	12

Which 2 angels are exactly the same?

Colour this picture carefully, as a present to Jesus. Then you can give it to someone you love.

2nd Sunday after Christmas

YEAR 1

Thought for the day:
God's salvation is for all peoples and nations; everyone is eligible.

Readings
Psalm 89:19-38
Isaiah 43:1-13
Matthew 2

Aim: To teach the children about the dangers of Jesus' early life and God's protection through his family.

You will need colouring pens, scissors, staples and copies of the model pieces shown opposite. Also slips of paper with the names of different members of animal families – enough to cover the number in the group. First play the animal families game. Each child is shown a slip of paper which has on it the Daddy, Mummy or baby form of an animal. When everyone knows who they are they have to find the other members of their family by making the right noises. When they are a family, Daddy stands behind a chair, Mummy sits on the chair and baby sits on Mummy's lap!

Now praise God and thank him for our families, remembering each person we live with. Tell the children the dangers of Jesus' early life, and how he escaped because of Joseph hearing God's warning and rushing his family off – perhaps in the middle of the night – as refugees. (*Donkey's glory* by Nan Goodall includes a classic retelling of this episode.) Help the children to catch the very real danger and fear there must have been, and the support of the family in the time of danger.

Help the children make this stand-up model of the journey into Egypt.

2nd Sunday after Christmas

JESUS' FAMILY ESCAPE FROM DANGER

SPOT THE DIFFERENCE

There are 5 differences

Trace the way they went

Bethlehem

EGYPT

Why did the family have to escape?
The ⬥⬥⬥ followed the ✡ to find Jesus. They told King Herod what they were doing. ☒ was ✝ and decided to kill all the 👶 in 🏘. God warned Joseph of the DANGER and Joseph got the 🐴 loaded up, Mary held Jesus tight and the family escaped during the night. The ☾ and ✰✰ shone in the sky. They didn't stop till they reached EGYPT where it was safer.

Colour this picture and think how you might have felt on a journey like this with your family.

2nd Sunday after Christmas

YEAR 2

Thought for the day:
God's salvation is for all peoples and
nations; everyone is eligible.

Readings
Psalm 89:19-38
Isaiah 46:3-end
Romans 15:8-21

Aim: To help the children realise that God looks after us all through our lives.

You will need some pictures of people of all ages, from birth to very old. Also include some pre-birth pictures and a pregnant woman.

Give the pictures out so that each child has one, and work together to stand with their pictures in order, starting with the youngest. (A fairly civilised way of doing this is to pick one person at a time, deciding where they should stand in relation to the others, gradually filling in the gaps. A less civilised way is to see if the children can work out the sequence for themselves.) In either case you should end up with a line of children holding pictures which show a growing and ageing person. The pictures are now stuck down in order on a long sheet of paper, labelled: ALL THE WAY THROUGH YOUR LIFE, GOD LOOKS AFTER YOU. Read the parts of the Isaiah passage which promise this and use the pictures to pray for all the different age groups.

2nd Sunday after Christmas

I AM GOD, THERE IS NO OTHER

When God decides to do
something, he always does it.
He decided to rescue us from
sin and he did it.
He wanted to save all of us,
the whole human family,
including you.

We are ☐☐☐☐
L A in God's
Y ☐☐☐☐
M A
F

The word GENTILE means:- AT
PTERROSTOEN WIHTOR ILSH
NOONTO JAEL WHINSTHE
(cross out every second letter)

BUT!

Circle the odd ones out

Search for the message and colour it in.

Epiphany

YEARS 1 AND 2

Thought for the day: In Jesus we see God's secret plan revealed.

Readings
Psalms 2,8
Isaiah 42:1-9
John 1:29-34

Aim: For the children to look at different ways God leads us in our spiritual journey.

Beforehand set up the secret worship place, which is where the trail will end. It might be a large cupboard or under-stair area, a small vestry or even a tent. Whatever you decide, it needs to be out of sight when the children start their trail. Set the children off in groups on a trail, either inside or out, depending on the weather. Each group follows their own colour of stars, which are placed far enough apart for there to be times when the direction is uncertain until they look more carefully (rather like cairns on mountains).

Every group's journey eventually leads to the same finishing point. This worship area is beautiful. It may have flowers placed on a mirror, lights or candles (great care!) an open bible and a cross. Have a rug or blanket down on the floor and quiet music playing, and make the entrance low, so that they have to stoop to go in. The idea is to make it a secret place of wonder which they are led to find. Have a SILENCE notice outside, and make sure the children come in quietly. When everyone is crowded in, tell them quietly and simply how God led the wise men to find him; how he led John the Baptist to recognise him, and he leads us to find him as well. But we don't all come by the same route. God uses all the different events of our lives, and the different people we meet; he can use sad times as well as happy times.

Sing a worship song together that the children know well, and then pray for people who are going through different bits of their journey at the moment. Have music playing again as the children file out and colour this star prayer to hang up at home.

LED TO JESUS

Can you help the wise men to find JESUS? ☽
Join the stars!

```
F O L L O W E D Q J
A P B C F I E D R E
H D R G E S S I M S
X L A E M E N P Y U
B O E K S D E J R S
W G A V E E C H R S
S Z G C L T N O H U
Y T B Y F X I T V T
Z M A N D W T D S H
A N O R N Q G C K E
```

THE WISE MEN
FOLLOWED A STAR
AND GAVE JESUS
PRESENTS: GOLD
INCENSE, MYRRH.

1st Sunday
after the Epiphany

YEAR 1

Thought for the day:
God gives us the grace necessary
to reveal his glory.

Readings
Psalms 46, 47
Isaiah 61
Ephesians 2:1-10

Aim: To see how God's glory is revealed in Jesus and in our lives.

You will need a beanbag, some pages from a magic painting book, brushes and water.

Begin in a circle (or several if the group is large), throwing a beanbag to everyone in turn. Practise throwing and catching in a way that challenges each person's skill – both hands/one hand/under one leg etc. and work at improving individual performance. Then stop using the beanbag but pretend to carry on practising. Are we really getting anywhere now? No – we need the beanbag to practise beanbag skills! In the same way we need God's grace to practise loving; if we don't ask for that, or try to do the loving on our own, our Christian life will be just as empty as us pretending to catch and throw.

At this point have some prayer and a worship song such as 'Jesus, Jesus, can I tell you what I know' or 'I am a new creation'.

So when we do work in the grace of God, what happens? Give out the magic painting pages and watch the way all kinds of colours show up when we simply use water. In our lives, we will quite naturally show the colours of God's glory and the world will be a more caring, forgiving, happier place.

GOD'S GLORY SHOWS

Do you know what
GLORY means?

Fill in the letters from the reflection:

God's Glory is reflected

in us,   WHEN?

whenever   N
we are   V

and   D
                    K
          L
        N

completely brilliant

Spoil!

special and amazing

evil

full of beauty

full of wonder and joy

selfish

Colour in the
Scribble out the

1st Sunday after the Epiphany

YEAR 2

Thought for the day:
God gives us the grace necessary to
reveal his glory.

Readings
Psalm 46,47
Genesis 8:15-9:17
Acts 18:24-19:6

Aim: For the children to see the connection between Noah's story and baptism.

Start with a game which directs attention to the different characters of water. When you call WATER! everyone 'flows' around the room. At ICE! everyone 'freezes'; at RAIN! everyone jumps up and down on the spot, and at RAINBOW! everyone joins hands to make a semicircle.

Now tell the story of Noah, with children joining in various sound effects and actions. Go through the actions and sounds with the children first, so they can listen out for where they come in the story.

Then show some pictures of baptisms, including some of total immersion. Explain how everything unloving, bad and selfish is being 'drowned' and the person being baptised is being reborn to a new, fresh life in Jesus. This is what Jesus taught us to do. Talk together about people they know who have been baptised recently, and if possible show the children the font, with its lid off, and the things that are used in baptism.

Help the children to make this rainbow, which could perhaps be displayed in the baptistry:

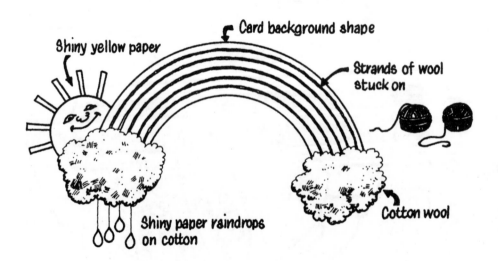

Shiny yellow paper

Card background shape

Strands of wool stuck on

Cotton wool

Shiny paper raindrops on cotton

GOD GIVES US WHAT WE NEED TO BE LIKE HIM

How can we reflect God's love?

When we are
KIND
PATIENT
FAITHFUL
FRIENDLY
HONEST

Complete the reflection

Draw another like this:

No, we can't. But Jesus gives the

			G	R	A	C	E

to live lovingly (yes, even YOU!)

Can we do this on our own?

YES NO

2nd Sunday
after the Epiphany

YEAR 1

Thought for the day:
God calls his disciples to spread the
good news of the Kingdom, whether
the people listen or not.

Readings
Psalm 15,16
Ezekiel 2:1-7;3:4-11
Matthew 10:1-22

Aim: To teach the children about the instructions Jesus gave when he sent the disciples out.

Prepare a few cards with instructions on, such as: 'walk round the circle and shake hands with everyone'; 'walk to the table and find the biscuits, then offer one to the people wearing blue'; 'hop round and offer a biscuit to everyone else'.

Now read or tell the children the story of Jesus sending his disciples out, counting up the number of disciples and writing each instruction on a board or flip chart. Talk together about why these instructions were given.

Make these drawstring purses with a prayer on the coins.

SPREAD THE GOOD NEWS

Find these words:
I AM SENDING YOU
OUT AS SHEEP AMONG
HUNGRY WOLVES

I	A	M					
B	T	J	F				
S	H	E	E	P	H		
S	E	N	D	I	N	G	
H	U	N	G	R	Y	I	M
A	M	O	N	G	C	G	P
W	O	L	V	E	S	N	
Y	E	R	X	C	J	Q	
O	K	W	O	U	J	V	
U	T	S	D	L			
O	U	T					
A	S						

When God calls us we have to

Who are we going to tell about Jesus being alive and loving us?

no one

everyone

only those who like us

only those we like

NO   NO

NO   NO   YES

2nd Sunday after the Epiphany

YEAR 2

Thought for the day:
Our God is a God
of wonders, and
it shows.

Readings
Psalms 15,16
1 Kings 20:1-29
Matthew 13:44-end

Aim: To familiarise the children with the 1 Kings passage, relating it to their own experience.

The narrative is excellent for telling and understanding through acting out. Make a mock up of a television for the narrator to speak through, and direct the action like a news, or documentary programme, with the different groups of people frozen in battle positions and moving whenever their part of the action is referred to.

Then go through it again, with someone ringing a bell whenever a learning point is reached. The point is briefly discussed and written up, and then the action continues. I suggest the bell could be rung at the following points, but of course you may well be directed to notice other things.

- We sometimes find ourselves under attack, either from other people, or from nasty feelings inside us.
- We think if we give in a little, the temptations will go away.
- They don't.
- It's a good idea to ask some wise people for advice when we're in trouble.
- Sharing the trouble gives us courage.
- God is fighting our battles against evil, so we are strong in his strength.
- God doesn't always sort things out in the way we might expect.

2nd Sunday after Epiphany

OUR GOD IS WONDERFUL

Can you love? Can you be kind? Can you forgive people?
Can you think? Can you have good ideas!

If so, then you are behaving like GOD!

God

we

thank

do

More

can

much

loves you

he also

and

think

Tick which ones you can do:

Draw yourself doing something clever.

3rd Sunday after the Epiphany

YEAR 1

Thought for the day:
God reveals himself through
signs and wonders.

Readings
Psalm 135 or 136
Isaiah 26:1-9
John 4:43-end

Help the children make some sweets which look quite ordinary but have a surprise in the centre.

Aim: To help the children recognise Jesus' glory through his signs.

You will need some ready-made icing mixture and a variety of fillings, such as chocolate drops, hundreds and thousands, or cherries.

First play the 'Who am I?' game.

Ask a volunteer to come and help. Secretly show them the picture of what they are and then hang the picture on their back so that no one can see it. Invite everyone to ask the volunteer questions to which s/he can only answer 'yes' or 'no'. Keep track of what is found out until eventually the identity is guessed correctly and the volunteer turns round to reveal that s/he is indeed who they thought.

An alternative version of this is to ask the children to guess by gradually adding dressing up clues to the volunteer, such as whiskers, tail and ears until the identity is revealed.

Now tell the story of healing when Jesus didn't even actually touch the man's son, and notice how the man is convinced when he realises the timing of the boy's recovery. Point out our need to look if we are to see God's glory at work in our lives and pray about this.

3rd Sunday after Epiphany

Follow the Signs

Who is this?
Follow the tracks
to find out.

If we follow Jesus we will find out what he is like. Here is one thing he did:
JESUS MADE PEOPLE BETTER

Jesus loved the good people and the bad people

GOD made the world

He must be GOOD clever KIND POWERFUL gentle LOVING

What am I?
* I am an animal
* I have fur
* I have sharp claws
* I purr

What am I?
Draw it here

I am a cat

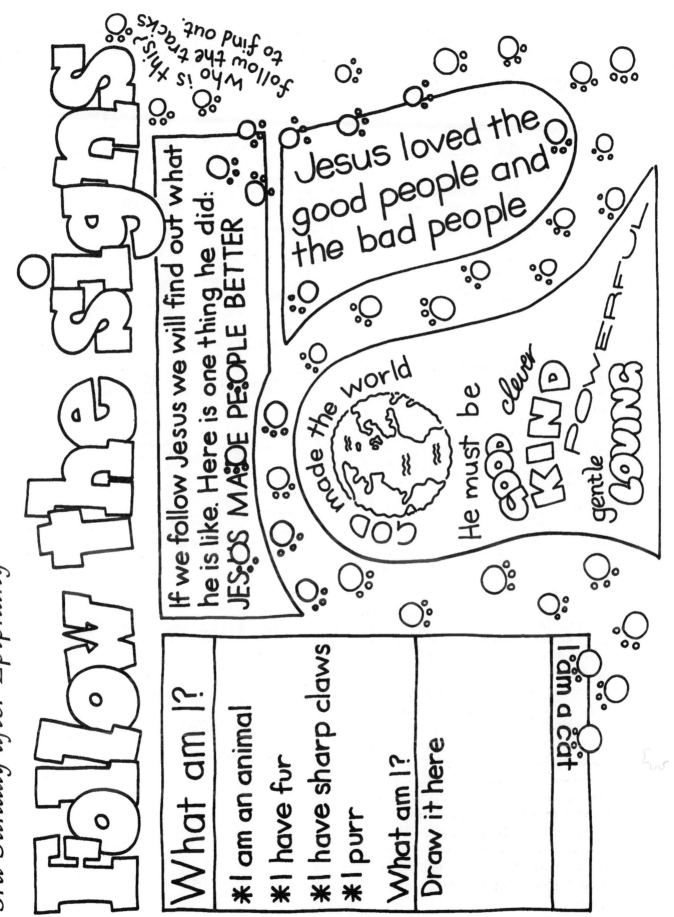

3rd Sunday after the Epiphany

YEAR 2

Thought for the day:
God reveals himself through
signs and wonders.

Readings
Psalm 135 or 136
Nehemiah 13:15-22
John 5:1-21

Aim: To help the children see the difference between keeping God's Law and not getting bogged down in petty rules.

You will need two large cartons and some strips of card about as long as the boxes are tall. Beforehand cover the boxes on one side and write out the summary of the Law on them: *'love God'*, and *'love one another'*. On the long strips write things like: *Don't carry your mat on the sabbath; you must not walk more than a short way on the sabbath; you must do this; you must not do that.*

First sing the summary of the Law with actions as set out above. Have the boxes displayed, and then explain how all the other rules were added to the Law to protect it. The children can get these rules and lean them up against the Law, until we can't see it very well any more.

Now tell the story of Jesus healing the man on the sabbath and pause when he picks up his mat. What do they think the synagogue teachers will think about that? Point out how they had protected the Law so well that they had lost sight of its real meaning. Jesus swept away the clutter (let someone do this) to see the important part again.

Help the children make this model to remind them.

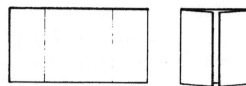

① Fold thin card like this

② Cut into the side flaps

③ On the middle section write and decorate the law

④ On the side flaps write 'Jesus shows us what is important.'

LOVE GOD, love one another

Spot the difference:

Can you see 5 differences here?

Match the pictures to the rules:

Why do you think these are good rules?

Because............................

Help the artist finish the picture of Jesus making the man better.

4th Sunday after the Epiphany

YEAR 1

Thought for the day:
God reveals his glory in the way
he rebuilds and restores.

Readings
Psalm 34
Zechariah 8:1-7
Acts 15:1-21

Aim: To help the children understand God's delight in restoration.

You will need something the parish needs mending, sorting out or re-covering (such as a notice board, an area of the churchyard, a general tip which could be a useful cupboard) and cleaning/repairing materials.

Tell the children about the people of Israel messing up their side of the covenant with God and eventually ending up as exiles. Link this with how we feel when we've messed things up and landed ourselves in trouble. Introduce someone as the prophet, who has a message for them all. (If this person is a clear reader, s/he can read out a simplified version of the prophecy her/himself. God loves his people and promises to restore them to their own country. His message makes people hopeful again. God doesn't enjoy punishing us – what he enjoys is helping us put things right.

Now tackle the restoration work yourselves, singing as you do so and enjoy working on it.

GOD HELPS US PUT THINGS RIGHT

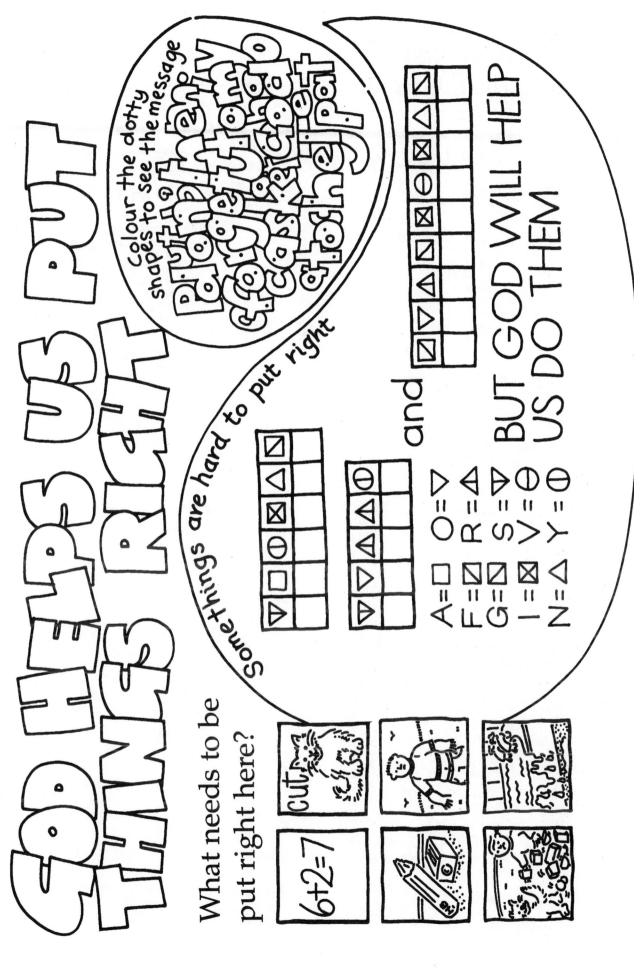

Colour the dotty shapes to see the message

Plum then... don't... un... forget to... for... ar... cask & God at... the... J Put

Something are hard to put right

What needs to be put right here?

6+2=7

cut

and

A=□ O=▽
F=⊠ R=△
G=⊡ S=▷
I=⊠ V=θ
N=△ Y=θ

BUT GOD WILL HELP
US DO THEM

4th Sunday after the Epiphany

YEAR 2

Thought for the day:
God reveals his glory in the way
he rebuilds and restores.

Readings
Psalm 34
1 Samuel 21:1-6
Matthew 12:1-21

Aim: To demonstrate how Jesus shows up what the law really means.

Start with a picture which you have covered with lots of pieces of paper, labelled with letters. Taking it in turns, the children ask for a letter to be removed, and they see how quickly they can discover what the picture is. Only when all the bits are removed will the picture be clear to see.

Remind everyone of the ten commandments, either in full or in summary of the law, and then have a couple of leaders or helpers being Pharisees telling the children some bad gossip about Jesus disobeying the law in various ways. (Eating wheat and healing someone on the sabbath.) What do the children think? Are the Pharisees right? It's true that Jesus did these things. Was he being disobedient to God's law?

When they have had a chance to think about that, read how Jesus answered the Pharisees' complaints.

Then let the children do this puzzle.

1. Colour in the dotted parts.
2. Cut these parts out.
3 Try to make them into Jesus' name on a plain sheet of paper.

70

4th Sunday after Epiphany

Jesus put things right

Love GOD and love your neighbours

What's behind there? The real law has been buried.
Can you fill in the bits we can't see?

Put a circle round the times we can talk to God.
Draw what you do at these times.

This isn't a very good picture, is it? Join the dots so you can see the hidden picture. Then colour it in.

What are the workmen doing?

....

5th Sunday
after the Epiphany

YEARS 1 AND 2

Thought for the day:
God's wisdom is that of a living,
powerful creator.

Readings
Psalm 119:121-136
Jeremiah 10:1-16
1 Timothy 3:14-4:10

Aim: To help the children understand the beauty and wonder of our God.

Have written out on cards the different truths about God, together with the false images people sometimes have about him. Throw the cards down on the floor and let the children sort them out according to what is true and what is not. Sing a song or hymn of praise together, such as 'O-O-O how good is the Lord', replacing the verses with the written truths about him.

Then help the children to make several banners to proclaim these truths, and display them in church.

Who is the real GOD?

Put red circles round the (true)

Put blue squares around the [false]

God is generous

God does what you tell him to

God picks on people

God knows me and loves me

God is pretend

God knows what is best for me

God doesn't like to see me enjoying myself

God is alive and powerful

Here are some things that God made

Write here the names of some people you and God love.

G	O	D	A	E	G	I	J
M	C	F	B	D	J	K	E
C	H	R	I	S	T	L	S
L	O	R	D	P	U	A	U
O	L	H	N	I	V	Z	S
Q	Y	P	R	R	X	C	B
S	S	A	V	I	O	U	R
T	W	Y	D	T	E	H	L

Find 6 names of God.

6th Sunday after the Epiphany

YEARS 1 AND 2

Thought for the day:
Jesus' glory is revealed in the
parables he tells.

Readings
Psalms 127,128,133
Isaiah 5:1-7(or 1-16)
John 15:1-11

Aim: To explore the nature of a parable.

First talk about secrets and keeping special things in secret places. Now tell them a parable – a story which has a secret hidden inside. (It's the story of the vine growing grapes and the branches that are cut off being unable to grow any.) Tell the story with a plant and good root system, either brought inside, or with the children gathered round a plant outside. Cut a branch off at the appropriate time.

Try and work out what the secret meaning of the story is. They may be able to think of the secrets in other parables that they know, such as the lost sheep.

Now help the children make this model of what a parable is which they can use to keep their own secrets inside.

You will need a box

Inside you will need cotton wool

and things to decorate it

PASTA TWIRLS

and spray paint

and a secret

6th Sunday after Epiphany

Stories with secrets

Jesus told stories
with secrets.
We call these stories:

Jesus is like a good shepherd—if we get ourselves
lost in life he will always come to find us.

Baa!
I'm lost!

I will go
and find
my lost
sheep

What's the secret meaning?

....
....
....
....
....
....

If we are cut off from God we can't grow in love.

....
....

Which branch will not grow fruit?

Why not? ....

What's the secret meaning? ....

....
....
....
....

BEFORE EASTER

9th Sunday before Easter

YEAR 1

Thought for the day:
Jesus teaches us by meeting us in our present situation and guiding us forwards from there.

Readings
Psalm 71
Deuteronomy 5:1-21
Luke 13:22-end

Aim: To look at the teaching aspect of Jesus' ministry.

Beforehand prepare two simple sock puppets tied with string to this script so that children will be able to read it

Cathy Dad, you know the hose pipe?

Dad Hang on, Cathy, I'm rather busy. I've got to get this garden watered before lunch.

Cathy But Dad, that's what I mean, the hose pipe is . . .

Dad Cathy I said I was busy. You run off and play.

Cathy O.K. Dad, but I wish you would listen.

Dad In a minute, love. Right, I'll just turn on and . . . AAAHHH!
The hose is leaking and all the water is making me soaked!

Cathy Yes, Dad, I knew it was going to do that. I could see the hole in the hose pipe.

Dad Then why didn't you tell me, you rotter!

Ask two confident readers to make the puppets act out the sketch, and then talk about how Cathy's Dad could have avoided getting soaked. Sometimes we could all save ourselves a lot of trouble by listening to one another better. Jesus went around talking to people and listening to them and explaining how their lives could be freed from all the guilt and fear which worried them so much. Lots of people listened and learnt from what Jesus said. He helped them sort their lives out. But lots of others were too tied up with their own ideas to hear what Jesus was really saying – they listened with a bit of themselves, but didn't really listen deep down, so they missed out. At this point the children can read the gospel reading from Luke.

Help the children make this jigsaw to complete before a certain time is up (depending on the age and ability of the children).

9th Sunday before Easter

A narrow gateway to heaven.

Why is Sam finding it hard to get through?

"I can't get through"

Find the words:

T	R	Y	A	E	T	P	I	Q
H	A	R	D	N	O	V	F	H
R	B	X	Q	D	H	H	O	E
O	O	C	W	D	O	O	R	A
U	C	K	E	F	R	J	G	V
G	D	M	N	S	L	U	K	E
H	Y	B	T	H	E	I	L	N
G	A	E	E	Z	T	M	E	N
N	A	R	R	O	W	J	O	P

TRY HARD
TO ENTER
THROUGH
THE NARROW
DOOR TO
HEAVEN

Here are some bits of luggage we need to put down.

This week I will try to…………………………………………

…………………………………………………

He has got so much luggage

9th Sunday
before Easter

YEAR 2

Thought for the day:
Jesus teaches us by meeting us in our
present situation and guiding us
forwards from there.

Readings
Psalm 71
Job 28 (or 9-end)
Luke 6:20-38

Aim: To recognise what God is like and see that behaviour reflected in people who love him.

First play a game. Work out the number of pairs of children there are, and mix up that number of pairs of animals – a parent and baby. Show each person the name or picture of one animal. Without using any animal noises the children have to act out their animal until they find their pairs. They carry on miming their animals until everyone is paired up. Suitable animals for this game are: rabbits, elephants, birds, kangaroos, snakes, lions and horses.

Explain how people should be able to recognise us as God's children by the way we behave. What do they think God is like? Write all the suggestions down in bright colours on a poster. (This is one of those times when you may end up learning more than you expected to!)

Have a lively praise song to celebrate God being as he is and follow it with a short 'sorry' time of quietness, remembering when we haven't behaved like God our Father.

Help them make a zigzag book by sticking a different quality of God's nature on each page. If there is time they can add others of their own.

Love your enemies

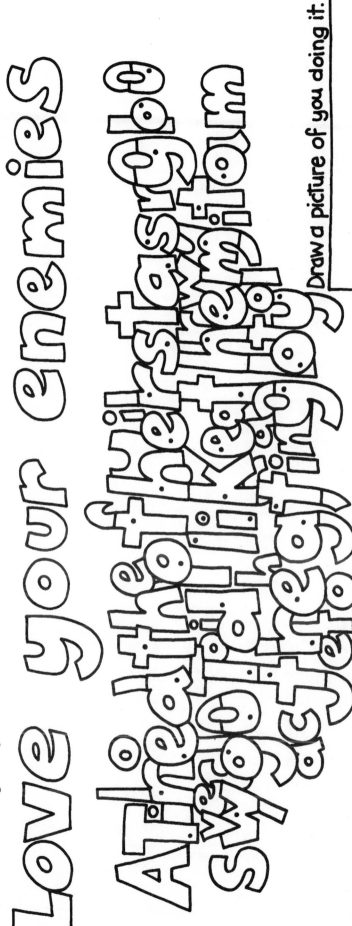

Draw a picture of you doing it.

Colour in the dotted shapes to see the message.

✓ The right way to behave
✗ The wrong way to behave

8th Sunday before Easter

YEAR 1

Thought for the day:
God knows us inside out.

Readings
Psalm 139:1-8
2 Kings 4:8-37
Mark 1:21-end

Aim: To teach the story of Elisha healing the Shunamite boy.

Start with a game in pairs. The idea is that one of the pair tries to be a mirror image of the other – by really concentrating on the other person you start to reflect them.

That's like us with God; when friends of God stick really close to him they start to reflect him and begin to behave like him. Elisha was a very close friend of God so he was able to let God's love work through him to heal this boy.

Now tell the story with the children acting out the different parts as you direct them.

Together make a cartoon strip of the story, with different children working on the main events:

1 The boy saying, 'My head, my head!'
2 The boy sitting on his Mum's lap.
3 Mum laying him on the bed.
4 Mum meeting Elisha and begging him to help.
5 Elisha breathing life into the boy.
6 The boy sneezing and feeling better.

Collect the sections and photocopy them into booklets to give the children next week.

8th Sunday before Easter

GOD KNOWS US INSIDE OUT!

What is your name? ....

What colour are your eyes? ....

What do you best like doing? ....

What makes you happy? ....

What makes you cross? ....

Can you remember being ill? ....

Can you remember the day you started school? YES | NO

GUESS WHAT—

XGXODXKXNEXWXTXHAXTXXAXLRXEAXDXY!

(cross out the crosses)

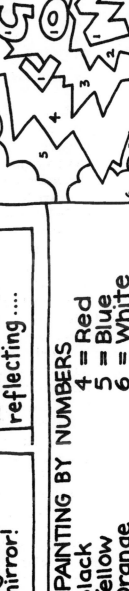

GOD'S LOVE

When we spend time with God we start to be mirrors, reflecting....

Draw what you see when you look in the mirror!

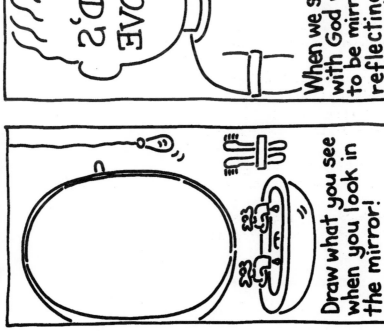

PAINTING BY NUMBERS

1 = Black
2 = Yellow
3 = Orange
4 = Red
5 = Blue
6 = White

8th Sunday before Easter

YEAR 2

Thought for the day:
Christ can make us whole,
but only if we let him.

Readings
Psalm 139:1-18
Numbers 21:4-9
John 9 (or 9:1-25)

Aim: To teach the story of the blind man being healed.

Begin with a game using your eyes, such as pinning the tail on the donkey or 'squeak, piggy, squeak'.

Talk together about how difficult it is when you can't see, and then tell the story from today's gospel, either using the floortiles method, or acting the story out as you tell it, with everyone moving to different parts of the room for the different parts of the story.

Then help the children make this model with moving eyes to remind them of the passage they have been hearing about.

Cut slits

Cut out eyes and nose

Jesus, 1 can see!

What would you miss most if you couldn't see?

°Think

What comes next?

Number the pictures in the order of the story.

Colour them in, now.

a bad temper   a shout   Friends

the sea   a horse   the wind   a ring

trees   happiness   SNORING

a football   OO

Circle the things you can see.

Can you see two palm trees which are exactly the same?

7th Sunday before Easter

YEAR 1

Thought for the day:
If you are a sinner,
then Jesus considers
you a friend.

Readings
Psalms 56, 57
Jeremiah 33:1-11
Luke 7:36-8:3

Aim: To think about what makes a good friend.

Use puppets to act out different situations where the children decide whether there's a good friend or not. Make some of these very obvious, such as comforting and sharing situations, but make some more subtle, such as a disagreement where the puppets argue and end up laughing. It is important that children realise we are talking about the real world and not some cloud cuckoo land. They need to know they can trust Jesus with their grumpy and angry times as well as with the times they are feeling good.

Make a list of all their ideas about what makes a good friend and point out how Jesus is all of these and more so: he is the best friend we could ever wish to have.

7th Sunday before Easter

Jesus is my friend.

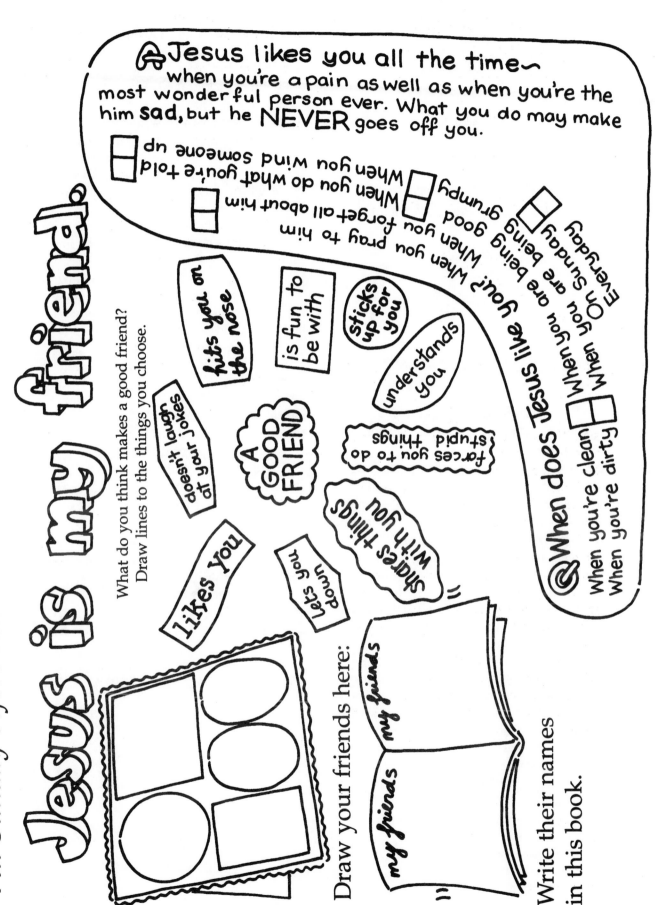

Ⓐ Jesus likes you all the time— when you're a pain as well as when you're the most wonderful person ever. What you do may make him **sad**, but he NEVER goes off you.

☐ When you wind someone up
☐ When you do what you're told
☐ When you forget all about him
☐ When you pray to him
☐ When you are being good
☐ When you are being grumpy
☐ On Sunday
☐ Everyday

Ⓑ When does Jesus like you?
☐ When you're clean ☐ When you're dirty

What do you think makes a good friend? Draw lines to the things you choose.

hits you on the nose

is fun to be with

sticks up for you

understands you

doesn't laugh at your jokes

A GOOD FRIEND

forces you to do stupid things

likes you

shares things with you

lets you down

Draw your friends here:

my friends   my friends

Write their names in this book.

7th Sunday before Easter

YEAR 2

Thought for the day:
If you are a sinner,
then Jesus considers you a friend.

Readings
Psalm 56,57
Jeremiah 30:1-3,10-22
Luke 13:1-17

Aim: To explore how Jesus gives us freedom.

You will need some lengths of rope, chain or thick string, a blindfold and a bicycle lock with padlock.

Tell the story of the crippled lady being healed on the Sabbath in the synagogue. You could do this by acting out the crowd watching, the Pharisees watching and Jesus calling out to the woman – she wasn't standing next to him. Look closely at the details in the account so that you get the real atmosphere rather than a clinical 'Jesus trick'.

Talk about how we often tie our lives up in knots. They may remember having done something wrong and then having told a few lies to cover up. Or there may be some who have once had a row with someone and now dread bumping into that person ever again. Those kinds of experiences are rather like pieces of rope tying us up and preventing us from moving freely. (Ask for a volunteer who will help by allowing you to tie them up here and there.)

There are other things which chain us as well. Pick out a really strong rope or chain and explain how selfishness ties us up and restricts our movement dreadfully – we're so busy thinking about ourselves, our own needs and wants, our own rights and so on that we can't reach out to other people at all. (Tie up the arms firmly.)

Arrogance and vanity make us think we're so wonderful that they stop us seeing the truth about ourselves (put on the blindfold) and fear and guilt can make us too terrified to move forward (tie up the legs).

So we end up spiritually trussed up, living a compromise and never living life as fully as we could.

Jesus loves us and hates seeing us like this; he yearns to set us free, and the good news is that he can. When we hesitantly let him into our lives he will start untying our ropes of selfishness, taking off our blindfolds of arrogance and vanity, unchaining our fear and guilt (do this with the ropes etc.) until he has set us free to live happily and love others. (The volunteer can caper around a bit to demonstrate).

Alternatively, play this game:

Divide the children into teams. One child from each team is caged in with chairs and can only be released by a special combination lock which the rest of the team have to solve. Whoever solves the combination code first and releases their team member, wins.

Here is the muddled message:

SET IN LET YOU AND LOVE FREE HIS WILL JESUS
which they must unravel to say:
LET JESUS IN AND HIS LOVE WILL SET YOU FREE.

God sets people free.

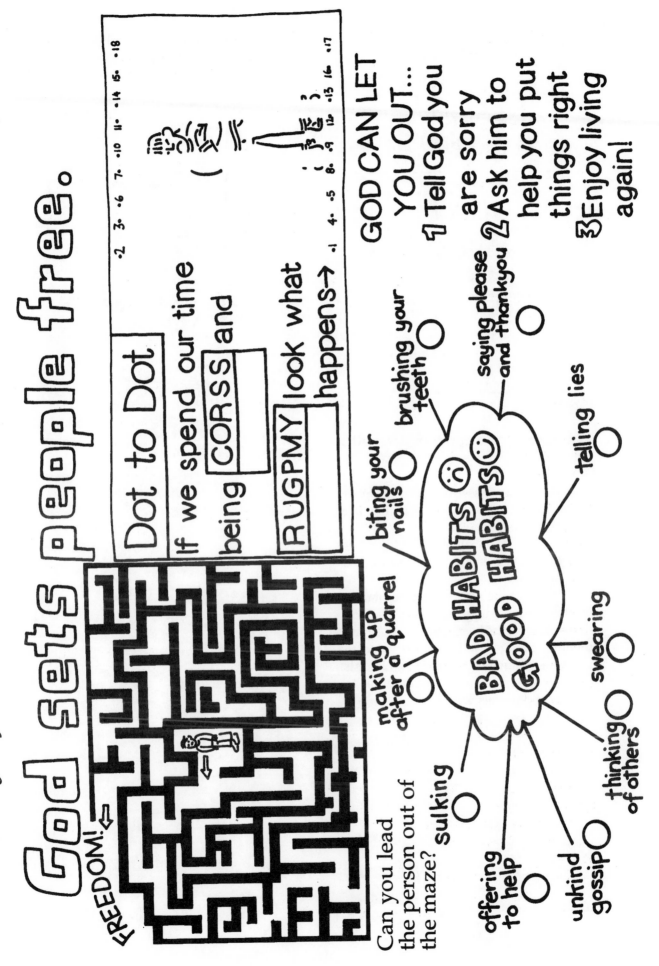

FREEDOM! →

Dot to Dot

•2 3• •6 7• •10 11• •14 15• •18

If we spend our time being CORSS and RUGPMY look what happens→

•1 4• •5 8• 9• 12• •13 16• •17

Can you lead the person out of the maze?

GOD CAN LET YOU OUT...

1 Tell God you are sorry
2 Ask him to help you put things right
3 Enjoy living again!

biting your nails ○

brushing your teeth ○

making up after a quarrel ○

saying please and thankyou ○

telling lies ○

BAD HABITS ☹
GOOD HABITS ☺

offering to help ○

sulking ○

unkind gossip ○

thinking of others ○

swearing ○

LENT

1st Sunday
in Lent

YEAR 1

Thought for the day:
We need to build up our defences
against temptation.

Readings
Psalm 119.9-24
1 Samuel 26
Luke 22.1-23
" 4 1-13
Exodus 17-1-7

Aim: To help the children deal with temptation.

Have ready a sword and a mug of water, and introduce the story by looking at these two objects.

Tell the story of Saul and David, either acting it out or using moving figures on a floor story mat.

Talk about the very strong temptation most of us have to get our own back on someone who has been nasty to us. Think together about how David managed to resist the temptation to kill Saul. Link his love for God with his determination to honour and respect Saul.

Help the children make this sword and cup to remind them.

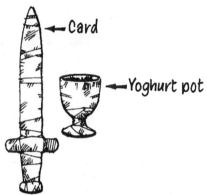

Cover the sword and cup with aluminium foil.

1st Sunday in Lent

Lead us not into temptation.

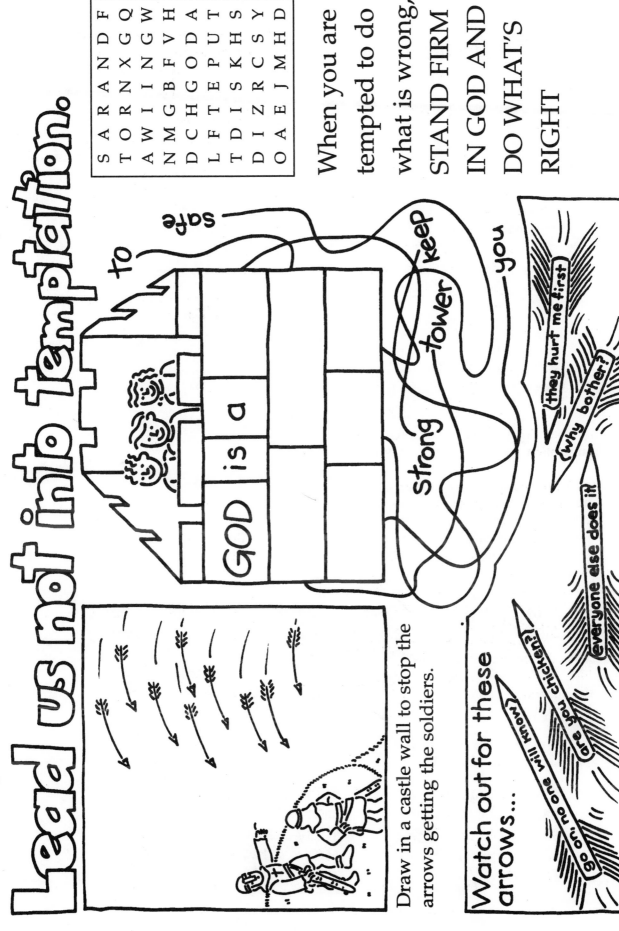

```
S A R A N D F
T O R N X G Q
A W I I N G W
N M G B F V H
D C H G O D A
L F T E P U T
T D I S K H S
D I Z R C S Y
O A E J M H D
```

GOD is a

to

safe

strong tower keep you

Draw in a castle wall to stop the arrows getting the soldiers.

Watch out for these arrows...

go on, no one will know?

are you chicken?

everyone else does it!

they hurt me first

why bother?

When you are tempted to do what is wrong, STAND FIRM IN GOD AND DO WHAT'S RIGHT

1st Sunday in Lent

YEAR 2

Thought for the day:
We need to build up our defences
against temptation.

Readings
Psalm 119:9-24
Exodus 17:1-13
Matthew 26:1-30

Aim: To familiarise the children with the Old Testament reading – water from the rock.

Begin with any group of songs which involve a lot of dancing about and aerobic actions (such as 'I've got that Joy' and 'Zip Bam Boo') so that everyone gets hot and thirsty. Have everyone sitting down and pour out some water for them all to drink, noticing how good it feels to drink water when you are really thirsty.

Now tell the story of the grumbling people of Israel in the desert and how Moses didn't grumble but went to God with the problem instead. That showed how much he trusted God, and God was able to help.

Talk together about the story and what it can teach us about talking to God about our worries instead of just getting angry and grumbling about things.

Help the children make this model of water coming out of the rock:

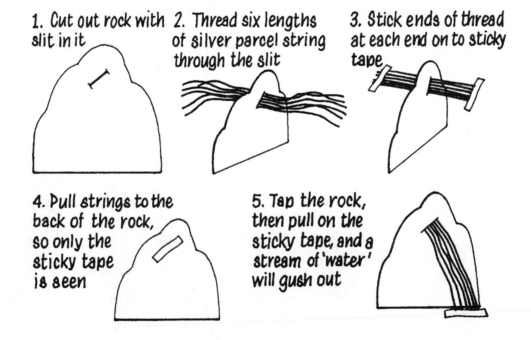

1. Cut out rock with slit in it

2. Thread six lengths of silver parcel string through the slit

3. Stick ends of thread at each end on to sticky tape

4. Pull strings to the back of the rock, so only the sticky tape is seen

5. Tap the rock, then pull on the sticky tape, and a stream of 'water' will gush out

1st Sunday in Lent

Lead us not into temptation.

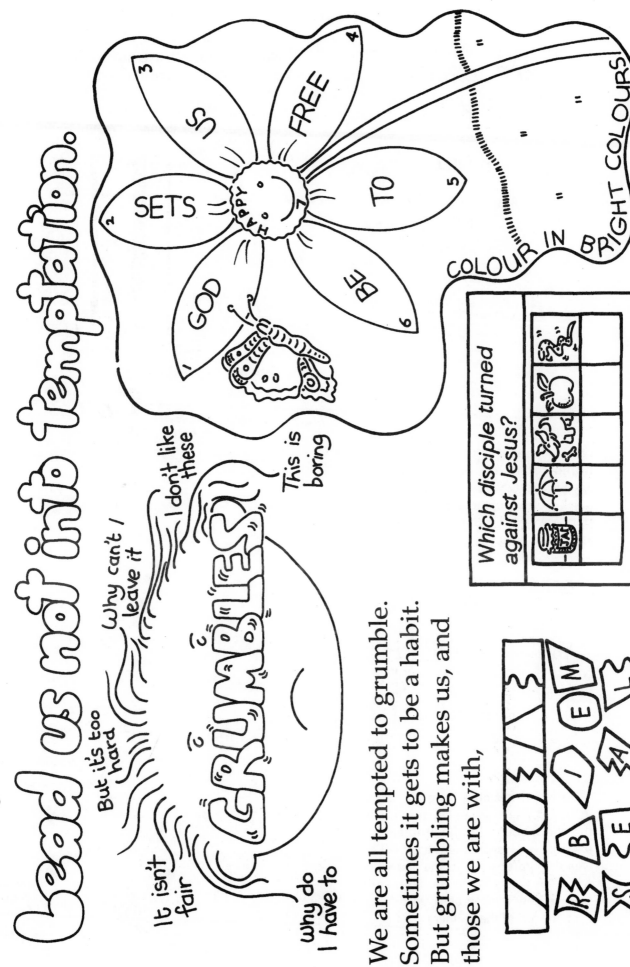

US

FREE

SETS

GOD

TO

BE

HAPPY

COLOUR IN BRIGHT COLOURS

But it's too hard

Why can't I leave it

I don't like these

This is boring

It isn't fair

GRUMBLES

Why do I have to

We are all tempted to grumble. Sometimes it gets to be a habit. But grumbling makes us, and those we are with,

Which disciple turned against Jesus?

2nd Sunday in Lent

YEAR 1

*Thought for the day:
Following Christ is not always a comfortable place to be.*

Readings
Psalm 119:73-88
Genesis 37:1-28
Luke 22:24-53 (or 39-53)

Aim: To teach the children the story of Joseph.

Tell the story of Joseph and his brothers, either with cut-out figures on the floor story mat, or, if you don't mind anyone seeing your awful drawing, draw quick sketches of the different parts of the story as you tell it. Simple figures like this are all you need.

Either draw on a long frieze or on different pages of a sketch book. Talk together about why the brothers hated Joseph, how Joseph might have felt as he was thrown down into the cistern, and when he was sold to the Ishmaelites. Look at how Reuben behaved differently from the rest of the brothers.

Now help them make this model of Joseph in his splendid coat.

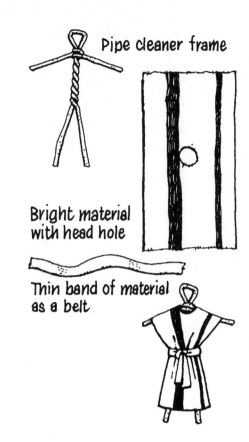

Pipe cleaner frame

Bright material with head hole

Thin band of material as a belt

let your will be done

↑Start here

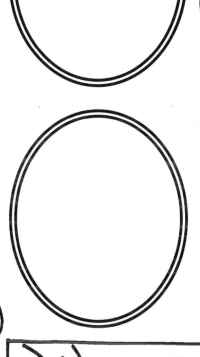

Draw (you) doing God's will when it is nice (you could be playing with friends, making a present for someone or feeding your pet.)

Draw (you) doing God's will when it is hard (you could be making up after a quarrel, sharing your sonic or helping with a job at home.)

He didn't enjoy being killed on a cross.

BUT

Jesus enjoyed making people better,

Start here

2nd Sunday in Lent

YEAR 2

*Thought for the day:
Following Christ is not always a
comfortable place to be.*

Readings
Psalm 119:73-88
Amos 3
Matthew 26:31-56

Aim: To introduce the children to the challenging nature of being a Christian.

Begin by daring some volunteers to do various things, such as singing a nursery rhyme on their own, walking round the church blindfold, or putting their hands into a bowl of custard.

Ask how many who are at school may be laughed at or teased for coming to church. (This is very common in many areas.) Encourage these people by recognising that they have been daring to come here today. Anyone who is teased or insulted at home or school or work for being a Christian is being brave, and Jesus knows all about their courage.

Then play the `What would you do?' game. Have a number of cards with situations on them. The children take turns in picking a card and saying what they would do in the circumstances. The others decide whether they think the person acted in the best way or not. No doubt you would like some ideas to start you off before you think of brilliant ones yourselves, so here they are:

1 You are playing ball with some friends and the new ball rolls into the road. You don't want the ball to be squashed by a car. What do you do?

2 You keep finding the person who sits next to you is copying your work. What do you do?

3 Your swimming training is booked for a Sunday morning. There is no reason why it shouldn't be later in the day. What do you do?

4 Your group of friends is teasing you because you are being friendly to a child they don't like. What do you do?

Now tell them how Jesus made himself unpopular by pointing out ways in which the religious leaders were misunderstanding God's Law. The leaders didn't like the way Jesus was friends with bad people, either, and they thought he was being very rude to call God his Father. So although he hadn't done anything wrong, but had stood up for what was right, they came to arrest him in the night.

We are followers of Jesus, and Jesus warns us that we won't always be very comfortable if we follow him. Do we dare follow him?

Help them make this secret agent identity card to carry around with them.

If the 'top secret' is in black ink
they can draw themselves in
pencil and it will still show

94

Let your will be done

You can choose GOOD.

Colour this in your FAVOURITE colours.

OR

Colour this in your WORST colours.

You can choose EVIL.

Cross out the YES and NO words to read the message:

JYESESUSNODYESIDNONOTYESCHNOOOSE
TYESHENOEASYESYWANOY. HNOECHYESOSE
TNOHEGONOODWAYESYBECNOAUSEYES
HNOELOYESVESNOUS.

Choices

Would you choose a ⚽ or a 🍦

Would you choose a 📼 or a 📖

Would you choose 🍕 or 🍟

Part of being human is being able to choose

3rd Sunday in Lent

YEAR 1

Thought for the day:
Christ had to suffer in order
to rescue us.

Readings
Psalm 119:105-120
Exodus 5:1-6
Luke 22:54-end

Aim: To teach the children this section of the Moses story, helping them to understand what was going on.

Beforehand prepare sufficient brick jigsaws for there to be one per six people. The completed jigsaws could look like this

Have the jigsaw pieces given out to each group or pair.

See which group completes their quota of bricks quickest. Time how long it takes for each group or pair to have all their bricks 'made'.

Now emphasise the impossibility of Pharaoh's command by giving the same task, except that this time the pieces of jigsaw are taken to different parts of the room before everyone begins, so they need to be collected before any brick making can start. Stop everyone at the time they completed the task the first time.

Otherwise give out beanbags and divide the children into equal groups. First they stand in circles with one person in the middle who throws the beanbag to each group member in turn. Next they have to take the same amount of time to do the same thing, except that they first have to find the hidden beanbag.

Now tell the story of Moses, Pharaoh and the bricks without straw. Have some words describing feelings printed on card and scattered on the floor. Have three hoops (or lengths of string) labelled MOSES, PHARAOH, and THE PEOPLE OF ISRAEL. Discuss how each might have felt, putting the word cards in the appropriate hoops. Some may overlap, like a Venn diagram.

Here are some suggested words to describe their feelings:
angry, depressed, lonely, irritated, threatened, selfish, determined, cheated, embarrassed, sad, puzzled.

BEING RESCUED MAY BE HARD WORK.

Now you try:

HARD → ☐ → ☐ → ☐ → WORK

Have a look at this:

BRICK → TRICK → TRACK → TRACE → TRADE

Only change 1 letter at a time.

To the rescue!

a flood

a cat in a tree

Draw in the rescues

a person down a hole

What did Jesus save us from?

HARD → HARK → PARK → PORK → WORK

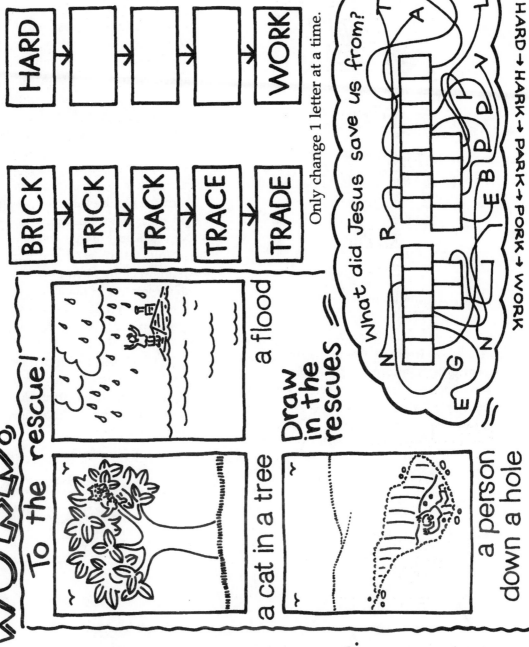

```
A  Y  B  I  S  R  A  E  L
P  W  H  C  X  E  V  H  I
E  D  A  W  A  S  C  O  F
O  Z  R  N  Y  C  U  A  E
P  V  D  B  T  U  J  R  K
L  E  P  N  E  E  A  A
E  E  Q  R  I  D  D  H  N
F  G  A  O  Y  S  A  P  G
G  H  O  G  R  M  M  L  R
F  M  O  S  E  S  T  D  Y
```

The PEOPLE of ISRAEL WANTED to be RESCUED. But when MOSES asked PHARAOH to let them GO, Pharaoh MADE LIFE VERY HARD for them. So the people were angry with MOSES.

3rd Sunday in Lent

YEAR 2

Thought for the day:
Christ had to suffer in order
to rescue us.

Readings
Psalm 119:105-120
Job 2
Matthew 26:57-end

Aim: To look at Jesus' arrest and persecution, addressing the question of why such a good person was treated so badly.

First show the children these messages and ask them to read them.

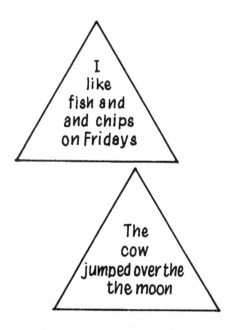

They will probably read them without noticing the repetition because they are not expecting it. We tend to see what we expect to see, and many faithful Jews expected Christ to be like another King David, leading his people to fight against the Romans so that they were free from Roman rule. Jesus wasn't like that, and talked about his kingdom in a very different way, so many people didn't recognise him as the Christ.

Now give out Happy Family cards and play a round of this game, where you can ask one person if they have a particular card and they have to answer honestly. Warn the children that in the story, Jesus will be asked a question, and you want them to listen out for what he replied.

Now tell or read the passage from Matthew, using pictures from a children's bible. Or a few of the young people could come and act it out in a simple way. Afterwards talk about the question Jesus was asked. He was under oath of the living God so he had to tell the truth. But they thought he was only pretending.

Now help them to make this three dimensional scene of the court and Jesus looking at Peter.

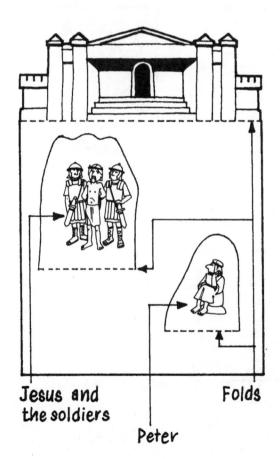

Jesus and the soldiers   Peter   Folds

Jesus was ready to suffer for us.

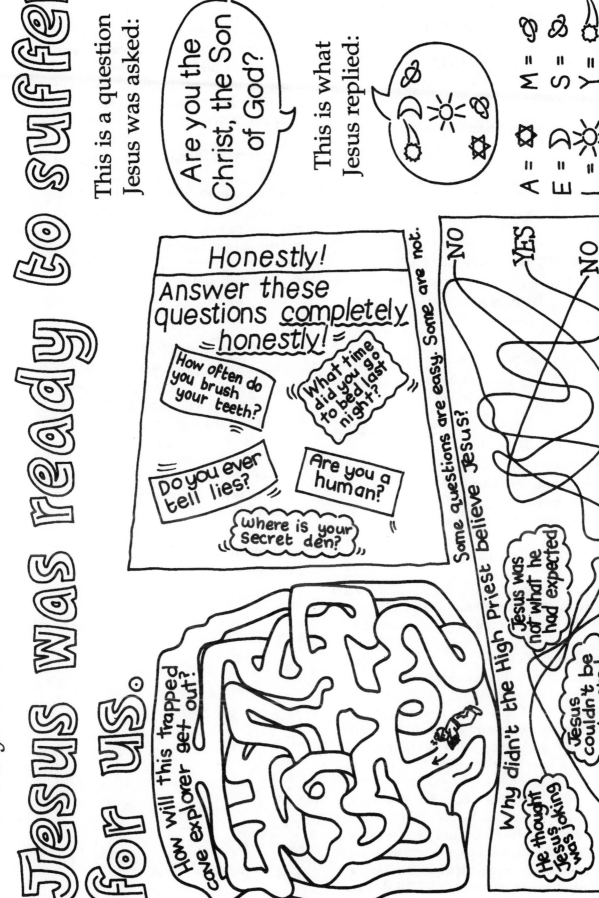

This is a question Jesus was asked:

Are you the Christ, the Son of God?

This is what Jesus replied:

A = ✡   M = ✆
E = ☽   S = ✆
I = ☀   Y = ☄

Honestly!
Answer these questions completely honestly!

How often do you brush your teeth?

What time did you go to bed last night?

Do you ever tell lies?

Are you a human?

Where is your secret den?

Some questions are easy. Some are not.

How will this trapped cave explorer get out?

Why didn't the High Priest believe Jesus?

He thought Jesus was joking

Jesus was not what he had expected

Jesus couldn't be trusted

NO

YES

NO

Mothering Sunday

(Also the 4th Sunday in Lent)

YEARS 1 AND 2

Thought for the day:
Just as our human mothers gave
us physical life, so God gives life
to our spirits through our
mother the church.

Readings
Psalm 139:1-18
1 Samuel 1:20-28
Luke 2:41-52

On Mothering Sunday the children are not likely to have separate activities, but they may be included in the following all-age activity. They could also make use of the worksheets during the service.

Theme: Counting the cost.

You will need a bucket, a ball of string, two full bags from the local supermarket, a pair of child's trainers, a cheque book and credit card.

Talk about what things cost, asking the prices of such things as Sonic, a Mars, a 5 litre pot of emulsion etc. Point out how the cost is known by those who have wanted or needed these things; our want or need pushes us to find out the cost so that we can work out whether we can afford it or not.

What about the cost of bringing up a child for a year? Let's check that out. It's something like 52 trips to Safeways (dump the shopping bags down) a couple of pairs of trainers, a chequebook full of club subscriptions, school uniform,

birthday presents and a holiday, and a credit card bill of petrol for the chauffeur service. But that's not all - it also costs an enormous length of patience (unravel the string up the whole length of the aisle) and 365 buckets of love, a fresh bucket for every day of the year.

If we look around, we'll find quite a few parents who are more than happy to pay that cost for the privilege of a year's worth of son or daughter! That's how God feels about us – he is glad to pay what it costs to set us free from our guilt and sin and worry and fear, even though the cost is incredibly high – rejection and ridicule, pain and death by crucifixion. That's a huge number of buckets of love.

Other ideas

• Many churches have posies of flowers for children to give to their mothers today. Make this a time of affection which leads on to a sharing of the peace, so that no one is left out, and all are shown God's love.

• Have two or three generations of one family to bring the offering to the altar and to lead people in the intercessions.

• Have one of the flower arrangements incorporating a lego house, and use bright, primary colours.

4th Sunday in Lent

MOTHERING SUNDAY

Join the right shapes together to see which mothers are which.

Cain's mother was

Joseph's mother was

Hannah

Jesus' mother was

Samuel's mother was

Rachel

MARY

EVE

I love my Mum because she...

Rose

Lily

Chrysanthemum

Freesia

Fill in the boxes with some of the kind, loving things your Mum does.

5th Sunday in Lent

YEAR 1

Thought for the day:
Jesus could only buy us full life by
submitting to full death.

Readings
Psalm 66
Lamentations 3:19-33
Luke 23:26-49

Aim: To help the children understand how brokenness and dying are necessary for new life.

You will need some jam jars, blotting paper, beans and water, and a jar showing a bean which has already germinated.

Read to the children the story of the crucifixion from a children's bible, *The Road to the cross* (published by Kevin Mayhew) or use one of the children's video versions. (Think carefully about what you use, as it is important that you have something which is suitable for your particular age group and experience – some of the excellent adult film versions are very disturbing for young or sheltered children.)

All the violence and pain directed towards Jesus is difficult to cope with, and it may help the children to see how beans have to break apart to allow germination and new growth.

Arrange the beans in the jars like this, and keep the blotting paper very damp.

— Damp blotting paper
— Water

After the beans have germinated they can be transplanted into the garden.

5th Sunday in Lent

JESUS DIED BECAUSE

HE LOVES US

Q. How can one grain of wheat feed millions of people?

A. If you plant it, it will grow about 30 grains. Each of those grains can grow 30 grains and so on....

MATHS

1 grain grows 30 new grains

30 grains x 30 = 900 grains

900 grains x 30 = 27,000 grains

27,000 grains x 30 = 810,000 grains

810,000 grains x 30 = 24,300,000 grains

24 MILLION, 3 HUNDRED THOUSAND in just 5 years!

Colour this picture of Jesus on the cross. He must love us such a lot!

5th Sunday
in Lent

YEAR 2

Thought for the day:
Jesus could only buy us full life by
submitting to full death.

Readings
Psalm 66
Isaiah 53:7-end
Matthew 27:33-54

Aim: To help the children understand how Jesus' death brought life.

You will need some packets of jelly, water and enough little pots for each child to have one.

Tell the story of the crucifixion using a suitable source for the age and experience of the children in your group. Talk together about it, being sensitive to reactions, as this can be a very disturbing time for some children. It is very important that the children see it in the context of the resurrection, and are not left after one session with the starkness and pain of the crucifixion.

Explain how often things need to be broken before they are transformed to something new, and let them all help making jellies, breaking up the cubes and melting them, so that they can be made into all sorts of shapes. If the jellies can be popped in a freezer for a while they will be solid before the children go home; for most of us, though, it will be a question of transporting them in liquid form!

FOR GOD SO LOVED THE WORLD...

Finish drawing the picture and then colour it in.

This is what God has for you

1
2
3
4

1. Someone forced to work for nothing.
2. What did Jesus die on?
3. Hot + buns are baked in this.
4. Finish.

Remember...
When you are ☐ or ☁ or ▷ ◁ is right ◁ ▷ you.
lonely
sad
God
hurting
beside

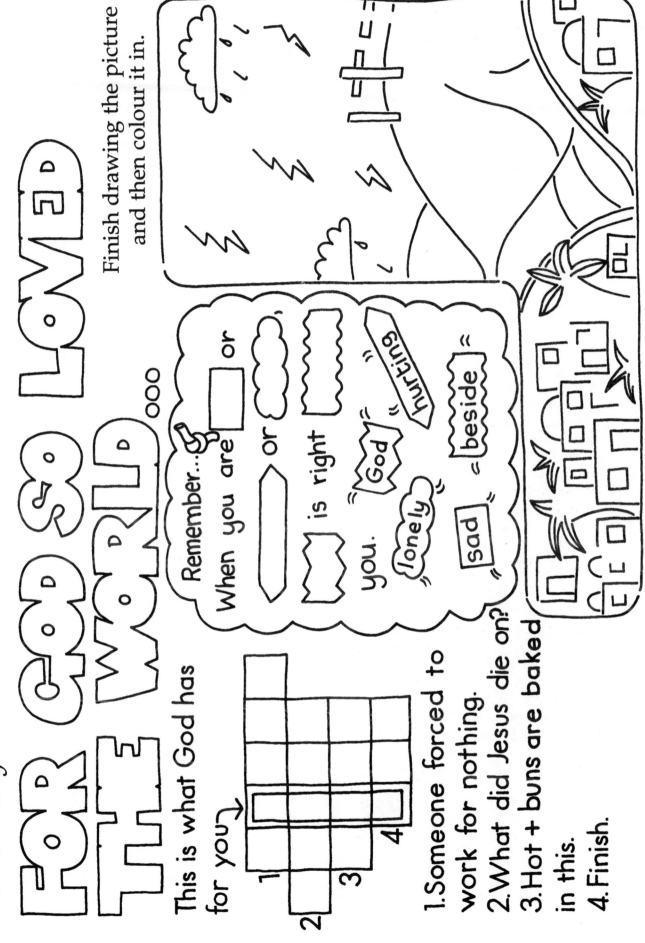

HOLY WEEK

Palm Sunday

YEARS 1 AND 2

Thought for the day:
The King of glory rides on a donkey
into Jerusalem.

Readings
Psalms 61, 62
Jeremiah 7:1-11 or Exodus 11
Luke 19:29-end or Mark 14

Aim: To see the contrast between the joy of the entry into Jerusalem and the anger of Jesus at the abuse of the temple.

First make these pom-poms –

1. Cut a handful of lengths of different coloured crepe paper

2. Fold it in the middle

3. Put two rubber bands on it like this

Then use them either in an all age procession, or in a time of singing and dancing on their own.

Then tell the story of Jesus throwing out the money changers, acting it as you tell it, explaining how the temple was being misused and then literally overturning a few tables and spilling everything on to the floor. The shock of seeing and hearing this really helps them realise the depth of Jesus' concern to put things right.

Palm Sunday

Hosannah! Hosannah! Hosannah!

SPOT THE DIFFERENCE

Draw in the faces in the crowd.

made

house

den

thieves

prayer

You

What did Jesus say to the money changers in the temple?

"My [ ] is a [ ] of [ ]

have [ ] it a [ ]

of [ ]"

EASTER

Easter Day

YEARS 1 AND 2

Thought for the day:
Death cannot hold the Lord of life.
New life for him means new life for all
who believe in Christ.

Readings
Psalms 113, 114, 117
Isaiah 12
Romans 6:3-14

Aim: To teach the children about the first Easter.

You will need a collection of those yoghurt pots which have two sections, some potting compost, pebbles and little flowers, small pieces of white cloth, and cardboard.

Tell or read the children the story of Easter, either using pictures, or moving everyone around to act out the story. Aim to get across the sadness which was suddenly changed into excitement and joy.

Now help the children to make a tiny Easter garden. If there is an area of garden round the church you can go and gather the pebbles, earth and flowers, of course.

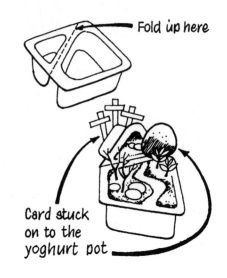

Fold up here

Card stuck
on to the
yoghurt pot

Jesus is risen from the dead

Stick this message inside card.

HAPPY EASTER

Fold

Jesus is alive for ever!

1st Sunday after Easter

YEAR 1

Thought for the day:
In Jesus we see the face of God, and
his risen life enables him to live in us.

Readings
Psalms 30,48
Deuteronomy 11:1-15
2 Corinthians 4:5-end

Aim: To help the children grow in awareness that Jesus really is alive today.

In your worship time, pray that the children will be made aware of Jesus' presence among us. Remind them of how excited Jesus' friends were when they found out that he was alive again, and talk about how he could suddenly be with them now, without even having to open doors.

Explain how we can get in touch with Jesus at any time of the day or night and he is always pleased to enjoy our company, whether we're happy or sad, muddy or clean.

To help them remember this at home, make these clocks.

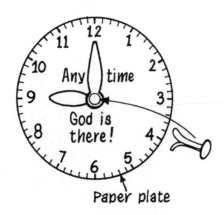

Paper plate

1st Sunday after Easter

Jesus is with us.

Who else has ever risen from the dead?

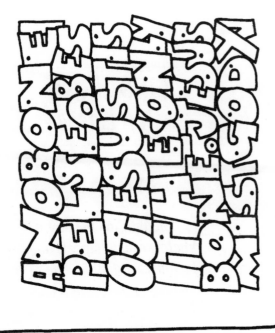

NO ONE
ELSE IS
JESUS IS
THE ONLY
ONE, JESUS
BONE, JESUS
IS GOD.

Can you see your own back?

| Yes | No |

How do you know you have a back if you can't see it?

| I can feel it | Oh, help— I have no back! |

Can you see Jesus?

| Yes | No |

How do you know he's here?

| I have seen him in the gospels | I see him in the lovely world |
| He helps me and listens to me | |

DOT 2 DOT

At first you can only see dots. Then you can see the picture.

Now ❧ ✿ L ✿ and point to where the ✿ goes. Open ✿ ✿. Are you right?

1st Sunday
after Easter

YEAR 2

Thought for the day:
Whatever may happen to us,
ultimately we shall be safe in the
hands of the living God.

Readings
Psalms 30, 48
Deuteronomy 4:25-40
Revelation 2:1-11

Aim: To show how God loves us through the good and bad times.

You will need two chalked lines to make a very narrow path which is hard to walk along, or one of those twisted wire contraptions from your May Fair which buzz or ring when you accidentally touch the wire.

Begin with everyone having a go at keeping on the straight and narrow and finding it impossible to do without a few slips.

Talk together about how it's just as hard for us all to keep to everything that is good and loving and generous and trustworthy and kind all the time. There may be some things which people find particularly hard, and it is worth talking through these honestly and lovingly.

The good news about God is that he doesn't give up on us or turn away in disgust whenever we do these things. He knows about them alright, and they make him sad, but as soon as we begin to say we're sorry, he forgives us. We are safe with the living God.

We are safe in God's hands

Colour the picture

What are these things?—they all keep us safe.

EEMHLT

ATES TEBL

FILE AJKCTE

KLOC

But we are not just BODY.
We are SPIRIT as well.
What keeps our SPIRIT safe from evil?

to see what is keeping Sam safe.

start

2nd Sunday after Easter

YEAR 1

Thought for the day:
'I bring life'

Readings
Psalm 49:1-16
Exodus 32:1-14
Luke 7:11-17

Aim: To teach the children the stories of the golden calf and of the widow of Nain.

Split the group in two, and help each prepare a presentation of one of the stories. They can act, mime or work with puppets. Then let each group show their presentation to the other.

Have a time to pray for the world – for anywhere they have seen on the news and want to pray for. It is helpful to have some pictures from the week's newspapers cut out and spread on the floor to help focus the prayer.

GOD BRINGS LIFE AND HOPE

What needs
sorting out
in our world?

_____

_____

_____

_____

_____

Draw and colour the
flowers which open up
after the sun and rain.

Can you sort out
the muddle?

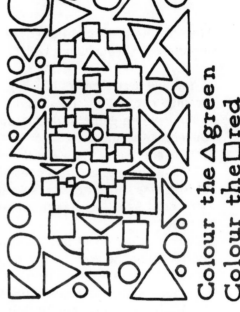

The person in
red enjoys
sorting out
the muddles
in our life
so we can
be happy again.

Colour the △ green
Colour the ☐ red
Colour the ○ blue

2nd Sunday after Easter

YEAR 2

Thought for the day:
'I bring life'

Readings
Psalm 49:1-16
Ezra 1:1-8
Revelation 2:12-end

Aim: To help the children see the importance of being honest with God.

You will need a ball or beanbag, and a dressing-up outfit of some kind.

First play a game of deceit, such as 'Queenie, queenie, who's got the ball?' (This is one the wrinklies in the church will remember!) Then dress one child up to disguise him/her as something different. Are they taken in by the disguise?

Talk together about how hard it is to deceive someone who knows us really well. God knows us better than we know ourselves, which can sometimes be a good thing, and sometimes not, depending on whether we're proud or ashamed of the way we're thinking and behaving. It's not worth bothering to pretend we're something different when we're talking to God because he's in on the secret of what we're really like. That means that we can be natural and honest with God, trusting him with what we are really feeling and thinking. Then, when we're open about the things we don't like in our way of living, God will be able to sort us out.

Help the children make this model to remind them that we don't need to wear a mask when we're with God.

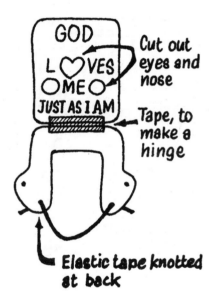

GOD LOVES ME JUST AS I AM

Cut out eyes and nose

Tape, to make a hinge

Elastic tape knotted at back

God puts things right.

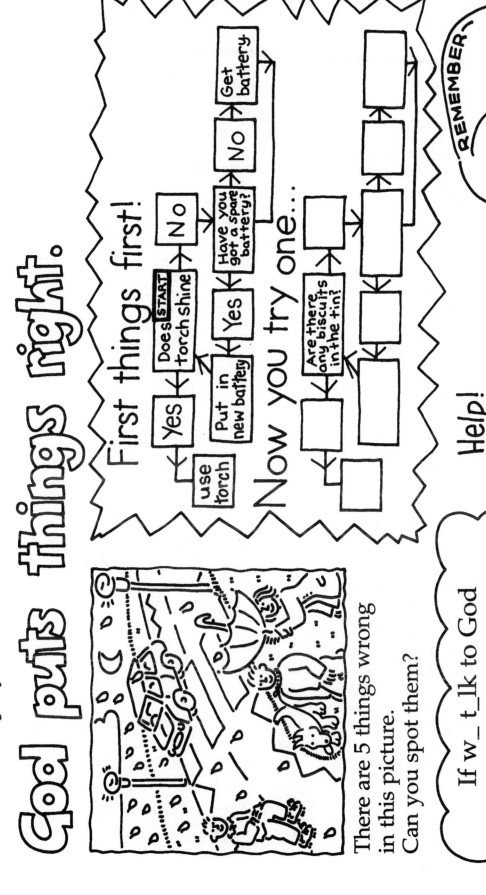

First things first!

START
Does torch shine?

Yes → use torch

No → Have you got a spare battery?

Yes → Put in new battery

No → Get battery

Now you try one...

Are there any biscuits in the tin?

There are 5 things wrong in this picture.
Can you spot them?

Help!
My typewriter can't type the letters e or a.

If w_ t_lk to God
_bout _v_rything th_t
go_s wrong, h_ will
h_lp us m_k_ it b_tt_r.

REMEMBER
Be honest with God

3rd Sunday after Easter

YEAR 1

Thought for the day:
Even if people don't believe in God,
he never for a moment stops
believing in them.

Readings
Psalms 121, 126
Numbers 22:1-35 (or 1-20)
Acts 17:16-end

Aim: For the children to learn to accept God as he is.

Begin by playing monster consequences. (Everyone draws a monster head, folds the paper down and passes it on. Now everyone draws a monster body, and so on.) Display the finished monsters and enjoy them.

There are also books available from libraries which have the pages split into three, and you can make your own combination picture of an animal or person. You could use this kind of book, or make your own by drawing three pictures, cutting each into three and letting the children make them up into different pictures.

Explain how people invent gods, and tell them the story of Paul walking through Athens and noticing the altar to an unknown god, then using this as a starting point to tell them the good news of the one true God.

Then help the children to make their own 'photo fit' kit. However they assemble it, the caption will always read the same: 'our God never changes'.

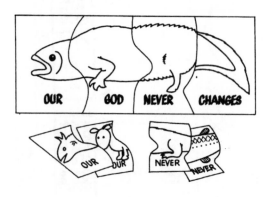

3rd Sunday after Easter

Our God never changes.

We make lots of things up BUT

we invent us already He because is God we can't invented He there

Have you seen him?

Draw what you think he looks like.

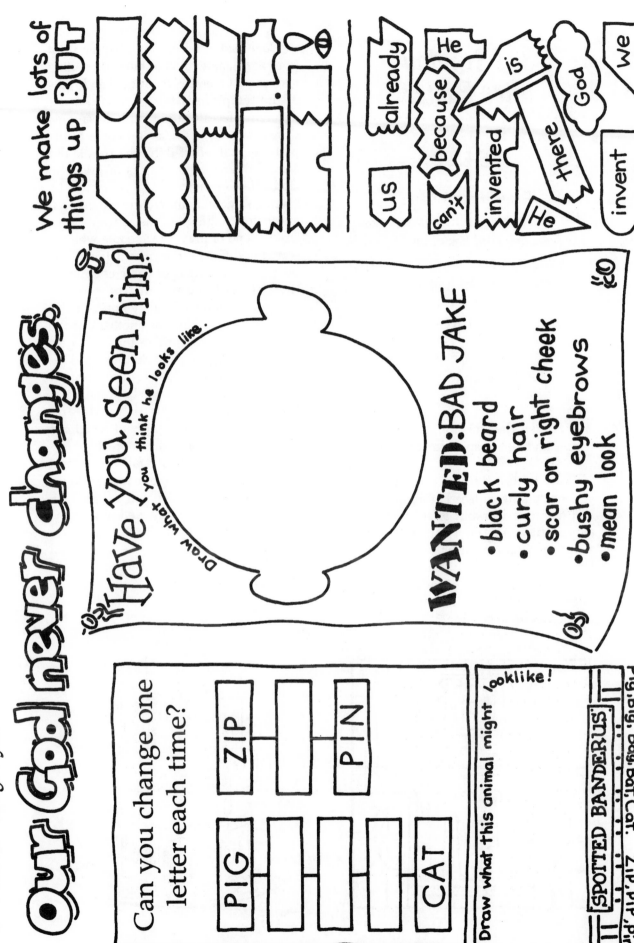

WANTED: BAD JAKE

- black beard
- curly hair
- scar on right cheek
- bushy eyebrows
- mean look

Can you change one letter each time?

PIG

ZIP

PIN

CAT

Draw what this animal might look like!

SPOTTED BANDERUS

Pig, Big, Bag, Bat, Cat, Zip, Pip, Pin.

3rd Sunday after Easter

YEAR 2

Thought for the day:
No matter how ruined or damaged our lives are, God has plans for a full restoration programme and is ready to start work straight away.

Readings
Psalms 121, 126
Ezra 3
Revelation 3:1-13

Aim: To tell the story of rebuilding the temple and look at spiritual rebuilding.

Start with a lively fitness training session, taking pulses before and after, and having a workout of such activities as running on the spot, stretching, stepping, skipping, sit ups, and jumping. Have a tape of children's praise music on as you work. Then have some quiet music as you talk together about building our bodies up to be strong.

Now read or tell the children the story from Ezra, about another kind of building and, as you mention the rubble and ruins of the temple, scatter on the floor the different pieces of the temple jigsaw (as shown bottom left). As you come to the part where the first thing the people did was to offer their sacrifices of praise to God, offer God some praise yourselves by singing something the children know well and enjoy singing enthusiastically. Also have a time of prayer for people who are scared of different things, as Ezra and the people were scared of their enemies if they started rebuilding the temple. (Children will often be very honest about this and can pray for one another.) As the rebuilding programme in the story gets under way, let groups of children work on the jigsaw puzzle – prepare enough jigsaws for there to be one between every four children. Sing with praise and thanksgiving as the people of Israel did when the foundation was complete.

Buildings eventually fall down, and bodies eventually die, but we can build our spiritual lives which will last for ever. How? The children may well have some good ideas which can be noted down. Then the children can make a spiritual building from junk to take home. It might look something like this:

God's rebuilding plans

How is this church being built? (write them in)

Draw a building using just these bricks →

Prayer

love for one another

Bible reading

leading good lives

people helping the starving and homeless

God leading us the right way

welcoming visitors

Build your life on GOD'S LOVE

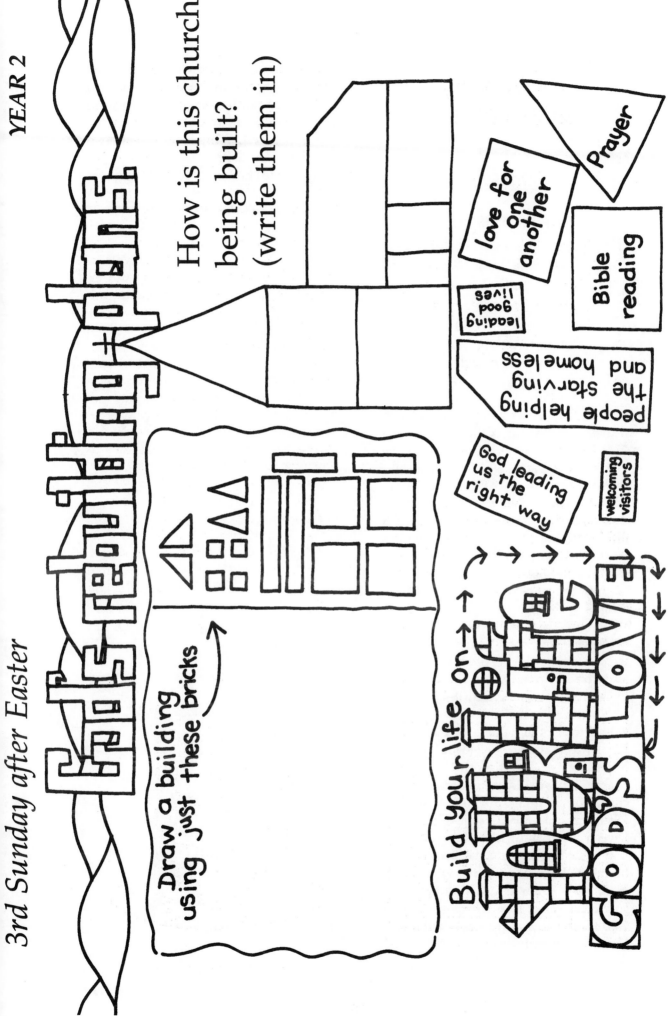

4th Sunday after Easter

YEAR 1

Thought for the day:
Prophets say what we need to hear –
not what we want to hear.

Readings
Psalms 57, 63:1-9
Numbers 22:36-23:12
Luke 16:19-end

Aim: To help the children learn to work with God at the helm of their lives.

First play 'traffic lights', where a caller shouts out either RED, AMBER or GREEN. If RED, they stop and sit down, if AMBER they crouch, and if GREEN they run about. Change the caller several times. Then talk about who was in charge during the game – was it the group leader, the ones who called out the colours or the children? (In a way it was all of these, because the group leader was in charge of the whole activity, the callers were in charge of what order to do things and the children were in charge of themselves in keeping the rules.)

Now read or tell the story of Dives, with the children helping you act it out. Dives was in charge of all his riches when he was alive; he thought he was in charge, anyway. Lazarus didn't feel in charge of anything. But they found out when they died that God was in charge. Dives wished and wished he had known that while he was still alive, because then he might have done things differently. Well, we *do* know that God is in charge, so we can make sure we spend time in God's company so we know what he'd like us to do in our lives. He won't push and shove; God hopes we will choose what is right, because he knows that will make us happy for ever, but he leaves us free to make our own choices between good and evil. Whichever we choose, God is still in charge.

Offer the children a choice of media to use to express the Dives story – perhaps crayons, paint or modelling clay.

4th Sunday after Easter

"God is "in charge"

we can choose

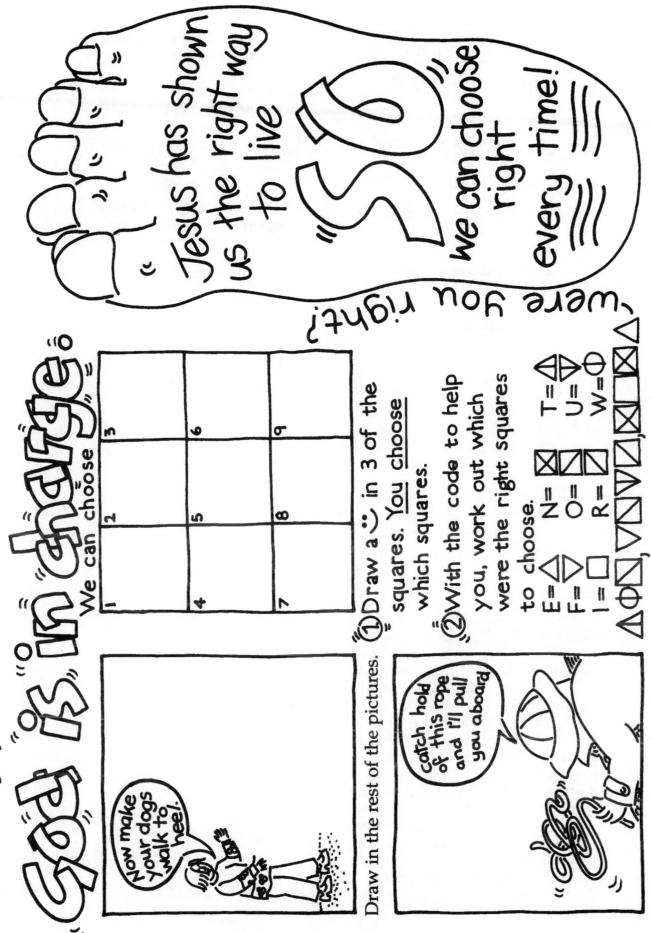

Jesus has shown us the right way to live

"So" we can choose right every time!

"were you right?"

Now make your dogs walk to heel!

Draw in the rest of the pictures.

catch hold of this rope and I'll pull you aboard

① Draw a ☺ in 3 of the squares. You choose which squares.

② With the code to help you, work out which were the right squares to choose.

E = △   N = ⊠   T = ◁▷
F = ▷   O = ◇   U = ⬠◇
I = □   R = ⬠   W = ◇⬠

△◇⬠▽, ▽□▽⬠, ◁△◇▽,
△◇⬠, ▽▽▽⬠, ⊠⊠⊠, △

4th Sunday after Easter

YEAR 2

Thought for the day:
God not only shows us the route, but
walks with us each step of the way.

Readings
Psalms 57, 63:1-9
Nehemiah 1
1 Corinthians 15:1-28

Aim: To help the children get used to the order of prayer first, action second.

First play a game of placing a series of pictures in order. (To prepare this game cut up some comic strips and stick each frame on card.) Talk about how important it is to get things in the right order; what a mess there would be, for instance, if I poured out the milk before getting my bowl of cornflakes, or tipped out the paint pots before going to the sink.

Now tell the children about Nehemiah, explaining how dangerous it could be for him to go and ask the king to let him go to Jerusalem. (They may understand this fear if they think of how they feel when they've got to ask permission for something from a very strict person who scares them.)

Nehemiah got things in the right order: 1) PRAYER 2) ACTION. Then God helped him say the best things, prepared the situation and everything worked out well.

You could also read to them a short piece from Corrie Ten Boom to see the same thing happening.

They can make this emergency card to carry in a purse or wallet.

EMERGENCY CARD
◆ STEP 1: PRAYER
◆ STEP 2: ACTION
...GET THE ORDER RIGHT... GET THE OR

God walks with us

plug in

pour water into teapot

fill kettle

drink cup of tea

get tea bag

pour out tea

Number the boxes so the story is in the right order.

Draw Nehemiah facing the King. Draw the King on his throne.

Then colour it in.

Nehemiah had to face a dangerous problem. This is how he did it.

PROBLEM ALERT!

STEP 1: PRAYER

STEP 2: ACTION

MAKE IT A HABIT

5th Sunday after Easter

YEAR 1

Thought for the day:
God is far more ready to lavish his blessings on us than we are to receive them.

Readings
Psalms 65, 67
Deuteronomy 28:1-14
Luke 10:38-11:13

Aim: For the children to become familiar with the Luke scripture and deepen their understanding of prayer.

Pin pictures or names of animals /people to the children's backs and set them off to find out who they are by asking other children questions about themselves. (No one is allowed to cheat by giving the answers away!) After a suitable time gather the children and ask each one what they think they are. Unpin them so they can see the full truth.

Talk about the way praying and reading the bible help us get to know what God is like and we'll end up knowing more about ourselves as well. Read the way Jesus taught his friends to pray, and go through the Lord's Prayer simply and clearly so that they know what it means. Use whichever version is most helpful to the children in your group.

Let the children draw round their hands and stick one section of the prayer on each finger, so that they can use their fingers to help them pray. Try this out together, with spaces between the sections to give everyone time to think about what they are saying. Emphasise the truth that they are talking to someone who already knows them well and loves them very much.

1 Our Father in heaven
   hallowed be your name.
2 Let your kingdom come,
3 let your will be done
   on earth as it is in heaven.
4 Give us this day our daily bread,
5 and forgive us our tresspasses
6 as we forgive those who tresspass
   against us.
7 And lead us not into temptation
8 but deliver us from evil.
9 For the kingdom, the power
   and the glory are yours
10 for ever and ever. Amen.

God likes giving presents

Here are some of them:

FILE

APLTEN TAERH

ERFE LIWL

LADY OFOD

F
W

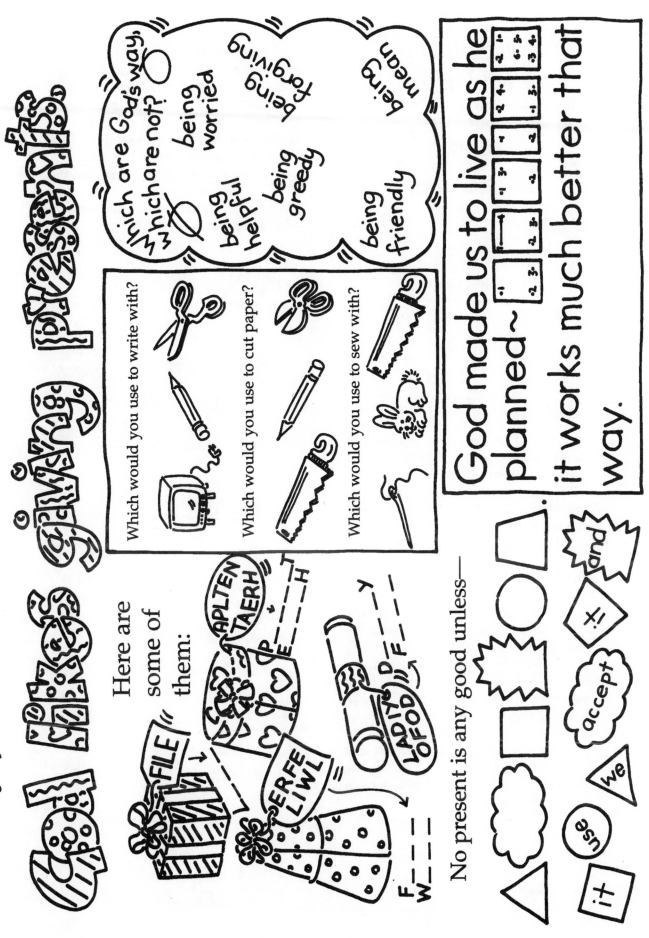

Which would you use to write with?

Which would you use to cut paper?

Which would you use to sew with?

Which are God's way, which are not?

being worried

being helpful

being greedy

being forgiving

being friendly

being mean

God made us to live as he planned~ it works much better that way.

No present is any good unless—

use
we
it
and
it!
accept

5th Sunday after Easter

YEAR 2

Thought for the day:
God knows best.

Readings
Psalms 65, 67
Nehemiah 2
Matthew 13:24-43

Aim: To increase the children's understanding of prayer as a valuable thing to do.

Start with a game which involves listening, talking and answering, such as the signature collecting game. Each child is given a sheet with a list of people whose signatures are needed – such as 'someone with red hair' and 'someone who has a green Ford car'.

Now read them the Nehemiah passage, asking them to stand up whenever it mentions that Nehemiah prays. Draw their attention to how Nehemiah is often praying inside while a conversation is going on, and we can do this too whenever we are in a tricky situation. Take a situation like facing a bully in the playground and act it out with two different characters, asking them to freeze every so often while everyone suggests the prayer that might be going on silently. Remind them that God can act to bring good out of the situation if we keep the channels open through prayer.

Now help the children make this prayer tree, writing their prayer concerns on one side of the leaves. Keep the tree going each week, filling in the date and outcome on the back of the leaves as the answers become apparent. Gradually the children will come to see how God answers prayer, and recognise that some answers take longer than others, and the answer is sometimes 'No' or 'Not yet' or 'This way is better', rather than always what or how we want it to be.

our prayer Tree

5th Sunday after Easter

God always listens

Draw what is under the water.

Draw what is under the ground.

GOD IS NEVER

TOO BUSY TO

LISTEN TO US.

G	I	X	T	O	W	T	J
G	O	A	H	J	Q	O	V
Y	N	D	B	B	K	O	T
T	C	F	I	U	M	S	I
O	U	L	I	S	T	E	N
Z	D	P	E	Y	L	R	G
N	E	V	E	R	B	E	U
D	O	C	A	F	H	I	S

Ascension and Sunday after Ascension

YEAR 1

Thought for the day:
Having paid for our freedom with his
life, Jesus our Saviour enters into the
full glory to which he is entitled.

Readings
Psalms 108, 110
Isaiah 65:17-end
Revelation 5

Aim: To help the children understand why Jesus had to go away.

Show the children what looks like a blank sheet of paper, but is in fact invisible writing. (You can use lemon juice for this or an invisible writing pen, widely available from toy shops.) Explain that there is a hidden message on the paper, but they won't be able to receive the message unless something happens first.

Now make the message visible, either by using the other part of the invisible writing pen, or by warming the sheet of paper with a hair drier if it is written in lemon juice. The word that emerges is POWER.

Go over the resurrection appearances and how the disciples saw Jesus going away from them so that he was no longer visible to them. We couldn't receive our message until something happened to the paper. The disciples couldn't receive God's power – the power of his Spirit – unless Jesus left them in that particular time and place. Now he would be available to every person in every country in every age, including us!

Let them experiment with writing secret messages and making them visible again. Then give them a fresh sheet of paper on which they write in invisible ink: JESUS IS HERE. This is one for their family to discover at home.

Ascension Day and Sunday after Ascension

Jesus goes to heaven

Purple

Pink

blue

white

Yellow

blue

green

orange

green

Yellow

orange

Red

Yellow

orange

Yellow

We can only be in one place at a time.

all

be

He

Now that Jesus has gone to heaven...

can

everywhere

once!

Where do you live?

_____

_____

_____

What school do you go to?

_____

What church do you go to?

_____

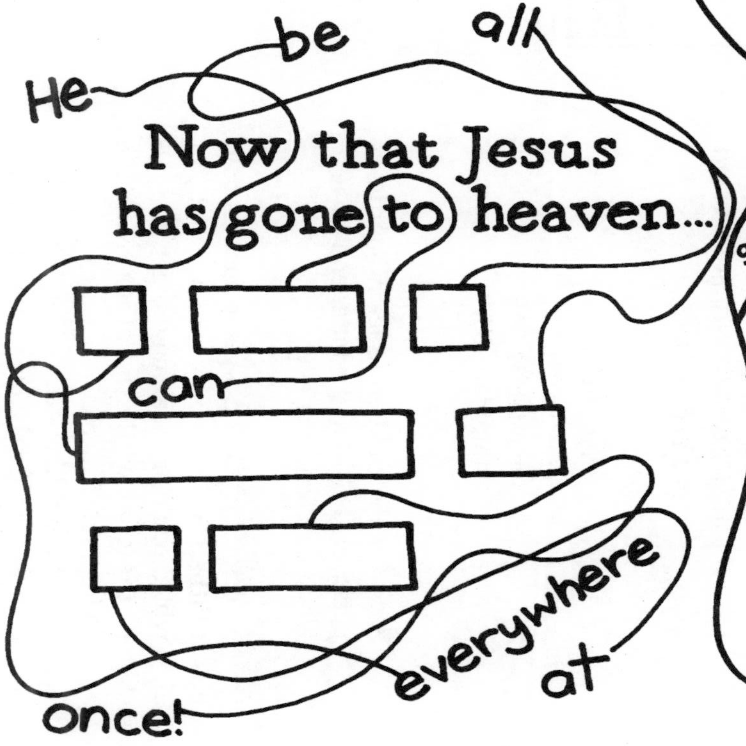

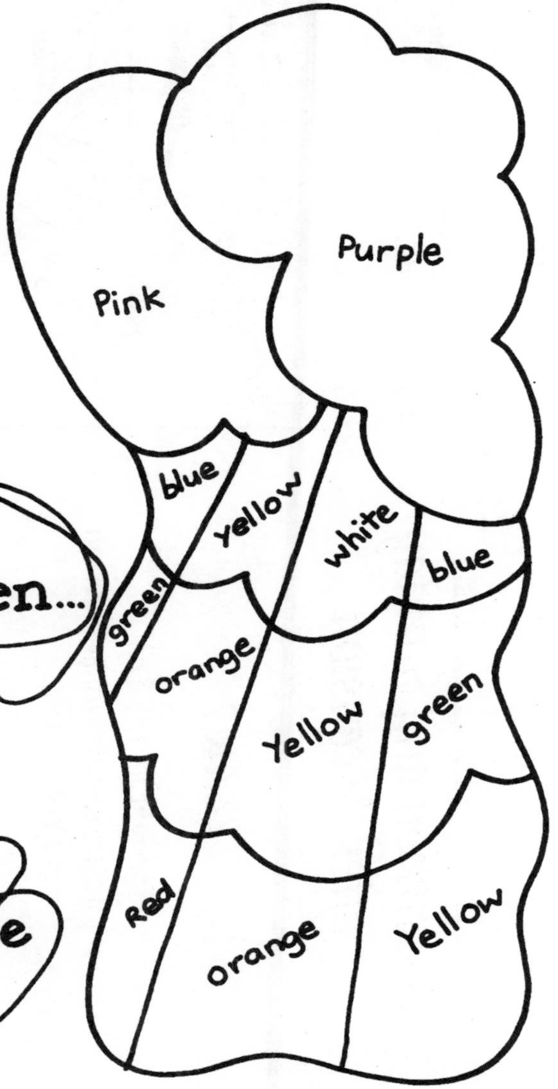

Ascension and Sunday after Ascension

YEAR 2

Thought for the day:
Christ's amazing humility is to be our perfect example.

Readings
Psalms 108, 110
Jeremiah 31:1-13
Philippians 2:1-8

Aim: For the children to learn how Jesus persevered right to the bitter end so as to win the victory over evil.

Begin by playing a game such as crab football or wastepaper basket-ball, in which one team is aiming to get through to the goal while the other team are trying to stop them.

Point out how games like this are like our life as Christians, when we are aiming to do what is God's will but it isn't always easy, and sometimes evil seems to be winning. Also, they may notice how the team members help one another, which is what happens to us – Christians and all the saints help and encourage one another along the way.

Now read the passage from Philippians, and point out how Jesus was not going to give up, however difficult or dangerous things got.

Help them to make this game to play at home to remind them.

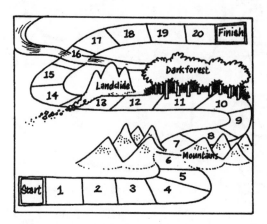

Ascension Day and Sunday after Ascension

Step by step, on and on

When?

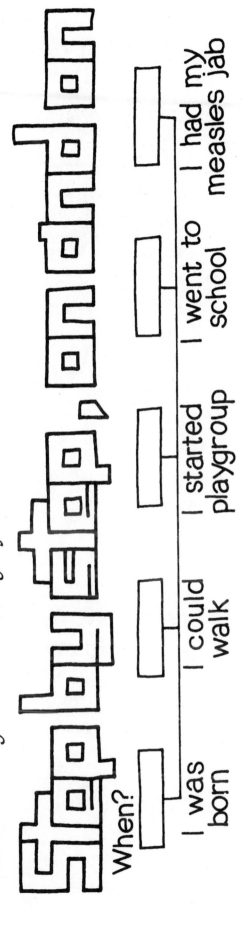

| I was born | I could walk | I started playgroup | I went to school | I had my measles jab |

* Jesus had put aside his glory
* been born as a baby
* died on a cross
* and come to new life.
  Now he returns to glory.
  He has saved us.

Draw Jesus going back to heaven.
His friends are watching on the hill.

Pentecost

YEARS 1 AND 2

Thought for the day:
When God's Spirit is poured out on
his people, it shows.

Readings
Psalm 68:1-20
Joel 2:21-end
Romans 8:1-17

Aim: To understand and celebrate what happened at Pentecost.

First help the children to make these streamers (see below) and then read or tell the Pentecost story, with the children using their streamers at the appropriate places.

Then have a lively time of singing and dancing, using their streamers and some of these songs:

Jesus is greater than the greatest heroes
The Holy Spirit sets my feet a-dancing
I am a new creation
We are one in the Spirit
(and there are lots of others).

Move from the lively praise into a time of worship, settling down and singing something like:

Jesus, Jesus let me tell you what I know
Father, we love you
All of my heart

Peg to fix crepe paper together. Tie string round peg, hold string and swing streamer.

Two lengths of crepe paper or ribbon

I will pour out my Spirit on all my People

R=red
Y=yellow
O=orange

Which holds most?

Number them in order

When the Spirit came to the disciples it looked like this

If someone comes to you hoping to find God's love, would they find your half or full? full empty?

If you want to be filled with God's Spirit, this is what to do...

God Ask him to fill you! turn to God

Trinity Sunday

YEARS 1 AND 2

Thought for the day:
God is creator, redeemer and life-giver
all at once, in every situation.

Readings
Psalms 29, 33
Exodus 34:1-10
Acts 2:22-36

Aim: To help the children understand more about God's nature.

Have a large sheet of paper entitled: 'What we know about God'. A long strip of lining or wall paper is ideal, and the larger the paper, the larger their writing can be. Sit all along both sides of the paper, with a variety of felt tip pens available. Talk together about what God is like, and have every right idea written down colourfully on the paper. If they need some help, see what they can work out from the way the universe is created, the way we are created, the way Jesus behaved and the way God's friends behave.

Have some quiet music playing as all the characteristics of God are read out in turn. Compare these with what Peter says in his post-Pentecost sermon and with what Moses knew of God. Phrases from the psalms can be used instead.

Using felt tips, stickers, or paints and photos, fill in the areas between the words, so that the whole sheet of paper is a blaze of colour expressing the character of God.

Trinity Sunday (Pentecost 1)

God is Father, Son and Spirit

2nd Sunday after Pentecost

YEAR 1

Thought for the day:
There's no better feeling than being restored to the God who loves you and to whom you belong.

Readings

Psalms 85,133
Deuteronomy 30:1-10
Matthew 18:10-22

Aim: For the children to understand Jesus' teaching on forgiveness.

Take the disciples' question – 'How many times should we forgive someone when they have sinned against us?' Work out Jesus' answer as a sum, and explain that this means every time.

Ask if any of them can remember having to forgive someone for something. It is important that children are allowed to talk seriously about such things, because forgiving is hard whatever our age, especially if the wounding is deep. If we are not careful, and talk too glibly about forgiving, they may assume it's easy for adults and feel guilty for struggling and failing. They need their leaders to be quite frank about how difficult it can be, and how we sometimes have to keep working at it. They also need to know that we can all ask God to help us – giving us the grace we need to enable us to forgive others.

Look at the guidelines Jesus gave us about forgiving in the lost sheep story by telling the story with some props or felt shapes on the story mat, and making a note of what we have to do if we're good shepherds. (e.g. Wanting things to be put right, making the effort to go after them or make the first move in patching up a quarrel, being prepared to spend time on them, and being prepared to get a bit bruised and muddy.)

Then the children can make a sheep each to remind them, using card and cotton wool.

2nd Sunday after Pentecost

Being found when you're lost

Being forgiven is a bit like being found

Draw in your face when someone says
I forgive you.

Q. How many times must we forgive someone?
A. 🐑🐑🐑🐑 🐑🐑🐑

E=🐑 M=🐑 T=🐑 V=🐑
I=🐑 R=🐑 Y=🐑

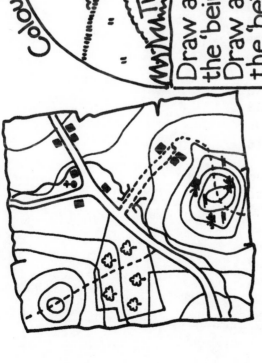

Colour the picture

This sheep is lost.
Draw a circle round the 'being lost' words.
Draw a square round the 'being found' words.

sad
lonely
worried
thankful
pleased

happy
fed up
scared
relieved
excited

Can you find:

1. A church with a spire

2. A muddy hill

3. A wood

4. A bridge over a river

5. A steep footpath

2nd Sunday after Pentecost

YEAR 2

Thought for the day:
In Christ we can all belong – he has broken the barriers down.

Readings
Psalms 85,133
Ezekiel 37:15-end
Ephesians 2:11-end

Aim: For the children to understand the meaning of Jew, Gentile and Christian, and look at who can be what.

First talk about the different surnames in the group, listing them as you do so, with all the different Christian names under the surname headings, so one family name may have several names listed. Play a game where everyone is moving about until you call a family name. Only the members of that family carry on moving, the others must freeze.

Explain that we are members of that family because we were born or adopted into it, and that when we read about the Jews in the bible, it means people who were born as members of the Jewish race which could be traced right back to Abraham. No one else could be a Jew, and God chose this people to work through. Through them all the other nations of the world would eventually be saved.

Have two hoops labelled 'Jews' and 'Gentiles' and explain that the Jews were God's people of Israel and the Gentiles were everyone else. Have some names written on small cards, and ask the children to work out where they should go. Suggestions for names: Abraham, Goliath, Joseph, Moses, Pharaoh, Jesus, Mary, Peter, Paul, St. Francis and the names of the children.

Now take the hoops and names away and replace them with one hoop labelled 'Christian – a follower of Christ'. Scatter around the hoop these labels; men, women, boys, girls, people with black skin, people with pink skin, people who go to (West Leigh) school, people who support (an approved) football club, people who support (a rival) football club, Jews, Arabs, Indian people. Ask them to put into the hoop those they think can be Christians, and leave outside those who can't. (This may be interesting.) Draw them to the realisation that *everybody* can be a Christian, whether they are born as Jews or Gentiles. Now stick all the names in place inside a large circle painted on a sheet of paper and label the poster:

EVERYBODY CAN BE A CHRISTIAN
IF THEY CHOOSE – NO ONE
IS LEFT OUT.

Pray together for the different peoples of our earth, using a globe or globe/beachball and passing it round as you sing, 'He's got the whole world in his hands'.

Jesus never leaves anyone out

3rd Sunday after Pentecost

YEAR 1

Thought for the day:
New life means revolution, and it can only happen through God's freely given power.

Readings
Psalms 11,20
Micah 3:5-end
Matthew 5:27-end

Aim: To look at how Jesus' teaching to love your enemies turns things inside out.

Show a quick clip of Tom and Jerry from a video, or some pictures from a comic strip. Why is Tom Jerry's enemy? How can they tell? Talk about other enemies they know about and/or have, and how that can be seen by the resulting behaviour.

Explain what the Jews had been taught about how to treat their enemies (hate them).

Now read the passage from Matthew about loving your enemies as well as your friends, which really turns our normal behaviour inside out. Jesus doesn't say we mustn't have enemies; but he does tell us to love them if we have them!

Give the children these bags to make, which turn inside out to show God's way of living.

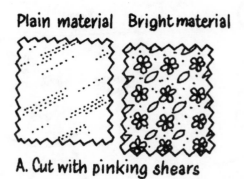

Plain material   Bright material

A. Cut with pinking shears

B. Sew together with dull fabric on outside

C. Turn inside out to show bright fabric

3rd Sunday after Pentecost

Love your enemies?

HELP!!

Write in here the names of people to pray for.

But enemies hate you~how can you love them?

But can give own
need love strength

On your ☐ you can't. ☐ with God
you ☐ because he will you the ☐☐
and you ☐☐☐☐ .

Draw in something for this person to hang on to, so they won't fall down.

WAY OUT

Draw some things to help these people find their way safely out of the cave.

3rd Sunday after Pentecost

We won't always want to do what is right. But Jesus will always strengthen us to be able to resist temptation.

YEAR 2

Thought for the day:
The kingdom of God is righteousness taking root in individuals and so affecting the whole of society for good.

Readings
Psalms 11,20
Isaiah 32:1-8
Mark 4:21-end

Aim: To introduce the children to the idea of our lives being under God's authority.

Begin by playing any ball/beanbag game where the rules are explained and kept to. Then talk together about why the rules were useful for everyone's enjoyment, and what might have happened if there weren't any rules. Tell them how good and well-disciplined they were to keep to the rules in the game, even when they wanted to cheat.

We have to train ourselves in self-control over little things so that we'll be able to stand up against temptation in bigger things (like drugs, alcohol or stealing). What are God's rules?

As the summary of the Law, sing these words as a round, to the tune of 'London's Burning':

You shall love the Lord your God with
all your heart and all your mind and
all your strength! All your strength!
And love your neighbour,
and love your neighbour.

This is even more exciting when sung with actions.

144

living as God wants us to live

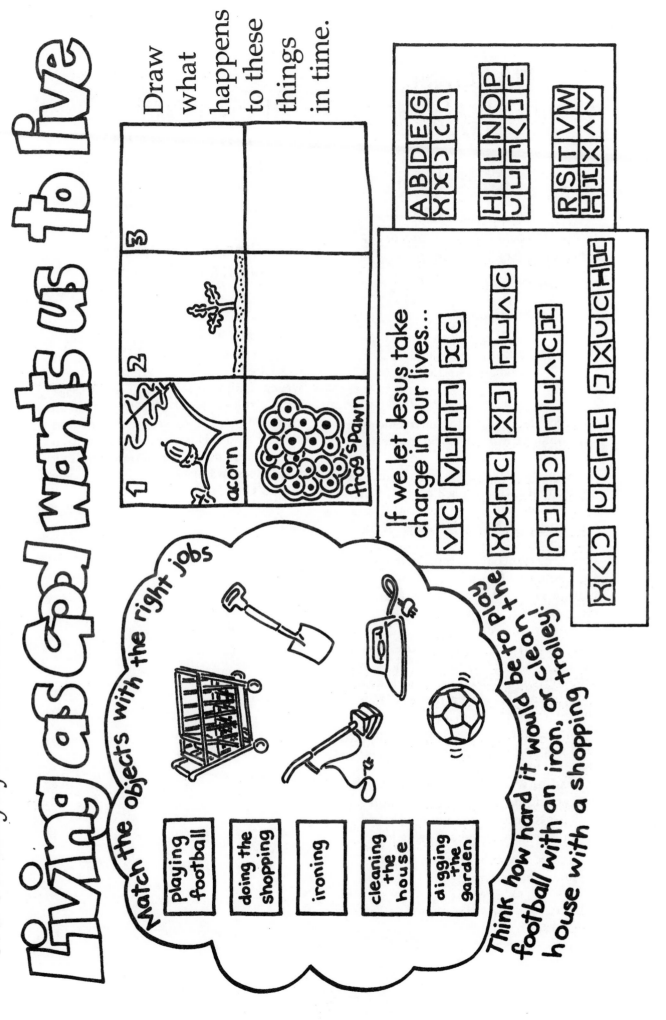

Draw what happens to these things in time.

1 | 2 | 3

acorn

frog spawn

Match the objects with the right jobs

Playing football

doing the shopping

ironing

cleaning the house

digging the garden

Think how hard it would be to play football with an iron, or clean the house with a shopping trolley!

If we let Jesus take charge in our lives...

4th Sunday after Pentecost

YEAR 1

Thought for the day:
True freedom neither means doing
what you like, nor being trapped by
someone else's sin.

Readings
Psalms 42,43
Ezekiel 18:1-4,19-end
Romans 14:1-15:3

Aim: For the children to understand that God wants us to be saved and not lost.

Begin by playing this team game. At the front of each team is a bowl of water and various small plastic containers, enough for each team member to have one. Some distance away is an empty bowl. The team have to transfer the water from one bowl to the other, using the containers. (This could well be an outdoors activity!)

Afterwards remind the children of how they tried to carry the water carefully because they didn't want even a drop to spill. That's how God feels about us, his people. He knows that if we choose to do what is evil in our lives we won't be able to enjoy everlasting life with God in heaven, and he knows how easy it is for us to choose what is wrong, instead of what is right. So God does everything he possibly can to stop us falling, because he loves us, and hates the thought of even one person being lost.

Explain how the people of Israel reckoned that children should be punished for what their parents did wrong, and then read them the passage from Ezekiel. Now help the children create this banner to explain the way God cherishes us. Have the hands drawn already, and then the children can draw themselves and place these drawings safe in God's hands.

Is freedom doing what we want?

God holds us safe. He loves us so much.

Jesus sets us free. Circle the things we can now do, and cross the things we aren't free to do.

laugh at people

stop feeling guilty

enjoy yourselfers

be happy the even when breaks car down

STEAL

forgive your enemy

be bossy

enjoy yourself

make people feel silly

So that we are free to LOVE LISTEN TRUST UNDERSTAND APPRECIATE SYMPATHISE

True FREEDOM sets us free from

guilt fear

all evil

Draw yourself, your family and friends safe in the hands of God.

4th Sunday after Pentecost

YEAR 2

Thought for the day:
God tells each of us our own story and loves us into his kingdom.

Readings
Psalms 42,43
1 Kings 10:1-13
John 4:1-26 or 1-42

Aim: For the children to know that in Jesus' eyes each one is special.

Start by playing the countdown game. Everyone stands up, and you say you're thinking of someone and they can find out who it is by asking questions. You can only answer 'yes' or 'no', and the one thing they can't ask is whether it's a particular person. The game is really a process of elimination, so if someone asks 'Is this person wearing glasses?' and the answer is 'Yes', then everyone who isn't wearing glasses sits down. Finally there is only one person standing, and that should be the one you were thinking of.

Talk with the children about how God knows all the details about us and understands us really well. That makes him the very best person to trust with our worries and secrets, our successes and struggles.

Give the children a copy of this chart to fill in, which they don't have to show to anyone at all; in fact one way of doing this is by asking them to go and find a place of their choice, either indoors or, if possible, outside. Tell them that when you want them back you will ring a bell. When you are all together again, ask them to hold their charts, containing their own special information, as you all pray in silence for one another, knowing that at the same time each is being prayed for by someone else.

My best colour is [ ]
My best food is [ ]
What makes me scared
[ ]
What makes me happy
[ ]
What I like best about me
[ ]
What I don't like about me
[ ]

4th Sunday after Pentecost

God loves us into the Kingdom

If you are meeting a friend off her plane, where will you go?

Jesus always meets us where **we are!**

Colour this picture of Solomon showing the Queen of Sheba his treasure.

```
Q A E G D I N K R I
S U Q O M P H I M M
N C E Q B R L N T P
L S H E B A U G V R
P G F W N I K D D E
Y F J H K S T O C S
J R C S Z E G B O S
V I S I T D W I S E
R E H X A I U P W D
S O L O M O N Y V X
```

The QUEEN of SHEBA heard that KING SOLOMON was very RICH and very WISE. She came to VISIT him. She was so IMPRESSED that she PRAISED Solomon's GOD.

5th Sunday after Pentecost

YEAR 1

Thought for the day:
If we really understood God's law it would drive us weeping to his feet.

Readings
Psalm 119:41-56
Nehemiah 8:1-12
Luke 11:37-end

Aim: For the children to hear Jesus' teaching to the Pharisees and look at real goodness.

Beforehand gather a collection of some real jewellery and some pretend. Display them carefully so that they look precious, and ask a couple of children to take them round and show everyone. If there are a lot of you, sing a quiet worship song while the jewels are doing the rounds.

Talk with the children about which they thought were worth most, and why. Then let them in on the secret that some things were in the 50p range, though some of them may well have been taken in by them. It would only be when they broke easily or scratched that you'd realise with disappointment that they weren't as good as you'd thought. Some people are like this too.

Now tell or read the story from Luke, getting the children to help you tell it by acting out the parts as you come to them. Explain first (and have them acting out) how fussy the Pharisees were about all the ceremonial washing; then they will notice how Jesus was far more bothered about the really important things than the rituals which were mainly just for show.

Then provide a number of different media so that they can choose how they want to express the story and teaching to the people in church. Some could act out the story in their own way, using the props from the teaching, some may wish to make a poster encouraging genuine Christianity.

5th Sunday after Pentecost

Goodness for show, or goodness for real?

The Pharisees started well, but they had got too

...about some things

and

How can we obey God's law?

Write or draw your ideas here.

Look at the picture and answer the following questions:

1. Is the girl holding a book?

2. Is the baby crying?

3. Is the washing up done?

4. Is the person reading the Bible doing God's will?

5. What would be better than reading the Bible at the moment?

...about the important things

5th Sunday after Pentecost

YEAR 2

Thought for the day:
God's saving news of love is not for a few, but for every person in every nation.

Readings
Psalm 119:41-56
Jonah 3 and 4
Acts 13:1-13

Aim: To look at some of God's surprising choices.

Start with a fast and furious game of choices. Label the corners of the room Tarshish, Nineveh, home and big weed. The children take it in turn to shout out one of these words and then everyone races over to that place.

Then sit down and retell the Jonah story with their help. Whenever you mention:

Jonah, they say: What me, Lord?

Nineveh, they say: DisGUSting!

Sailors, they get up and do 4 seconds
of a hornpipe,

Big Fish, they open and close their
mouths, fish-like,

and they make the appropriate noises when you say Wind and Sea.

Point out how Jonah was surprised and angry that God had chosen to save a place like Nineveh. We may be surprised at the jobs God chooses us for. He may need to use us at the shops, in the kitchen at home, down at the tip, in the middle of dinner or in the middle of a maths lesson.

Help them to make this moving model of Jonah and the big fish.

1. Cut two card fish and staple them together as shown
2. Cut a slit in the fish
3. Attach string to Jonah and thread through fish

Choosing as God chooses

Which chocolate would you choose?

How did the people in the early church choose Paul and Barnabas?

&

Why do you think Jonah wanted to save his weed?

N.B. To FAST means to go without food.

Why do you think God wanted to save the city of Nineveh?

HOW DID YOU CHOOSE?

Number the reasons in order.

☐ I had this one before and liked it.

☐ This chocolate looked as if it would be nice.

☐ I only like nutty/soft ones.

☐ I haven't tried this before and I like to try new things.

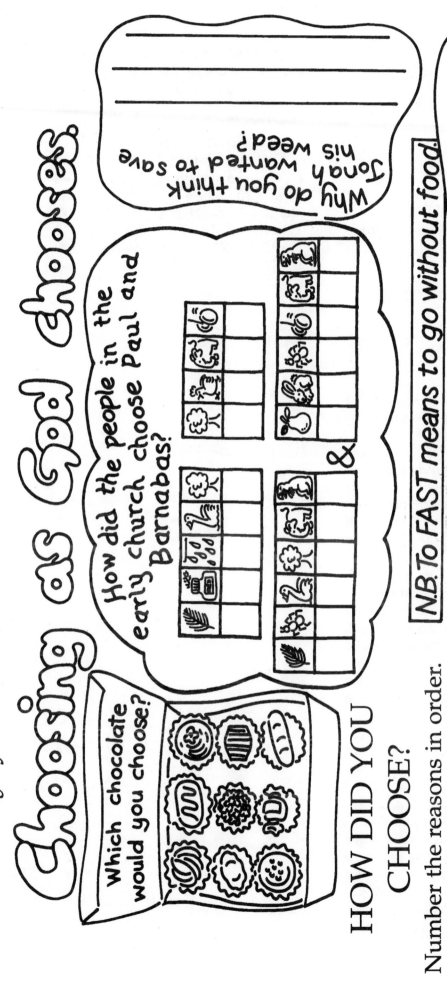

6th Sunday after Pentecost

YEAR 1

Thought for the day:
In Jesus we are not just patched up
but made new.

Readings
Psalm 77
Isaiah 43:14-44:5
Mark 2:18-36

Aim: For the children to know that God doesn't just patch up, but makes new.

Take the children on a journey, using different parts of the building and/or churchyard, doing different sections of the story and teaching in different areas.

Begin in Egypt, and get them to tell you the familiar story of the people of Israel as slaves. When you get to the crossing of the sea, lead them out through two lines of chairs to the other side, where you can all rejoice that you are free. Lead them on to the Promised Land, where you tell them about how the people didn't stay faithful to God, but messed things up time after time, until at last they were overcome and taken off to exile in Babylon. Move off to another area at this point. The people know that although God had kept his promise they hadn't kept theirs and they knew they had messed things up. Now read excerpts from the prophet Isaiah to see what God said to his people and how he gave them hope. Then take the children on a whistle stop tour over the same journey, explaining it in terms of a person: we get stuck in a bad habit like being lazy or selfish or telling lies a lot, and God leads us out of it, but gradually we find we're messing things up again until our bad habits hold us again like exiles. So God's words of hope are for us, too; in Jesus we can be gradually made new. He will sort out and heal the things that make us behave badly.

Give the children balls of clay and let them model something good emerging from a shapeless lump. Display the models with a sign: LOOK AT THE NEW THING I AM GOING TO DO. IT IS HAPPENING ALREADY – YOU CAN SEE IT NOW!

6th Sunday after Pentecost

Not patched up but made NEW!

Can you untangle the fishing lines—who has caught which fish?

What needs putting right here?

$$\begin{array}{r} 23 \\ +12 \\ \hline 36 \end{array}$$

I wos here

31st September

$2 \times 7 = 27$

There are 16

MANCHESTER

LONDON

Make a new picture by joining up the dots how you like and colouring in.

Do you need God to sort you out in any of these things? Think it over, and talk to God about it.

BEING LAZY Telling lies SULKING ARGUING BEING A BAD LOSER Being bossy

6th Sunday after Pentecost

YEAR 2

Thought for the day:
In Jesus we are not just patched up
but made new.

Readings
Psalm 77
2 Samuel 12:1-18a (or-23)
Acts 9:1-22

Aim: For the children to see how God sorted out King David's sin and can sort ours out too.

Start by holding hands in small groups and getting into a real muddle. Then, still holding hands, try to straighten things out. We're going to think about how God sorts our lives out when we get in a muddle.

Explain simply and clearly what David had done – many of them will be familiar with such events through watching the soaps. Then read or tell Nathan's story. What do they think of the way the man behaved? Tell them what David thought, and then how Nathan showed David that he was the man in the story. See if the children can work out why this was so, before going on to Nathan's words from God. Point out how David was forgiven as soon as he had said 'I have sinned'. Whatever we do wrong, however badly we mess things up, God will always forgive us.

Then help them to make this card with instructions for what to do in case of sin.

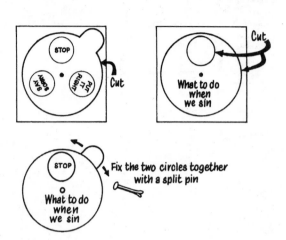

6th Sunday after Pentecost

God is an expert at putting things right.

draw the pattern on the wallpaper

Put these instructions in order

fill cracks in wall

hang paper on wall

cut strip of paper

paste paper

Scrape off paper

What to do when you SIN (act or think or speak or a way that makes GOD sad.)

1.
2.
3.
4.
5.

Stop

SAY SORRY

PUT IT RIGHT

Colour the traffic lights

1. Write your friend's name at the bottom of this page.
2. Write another name on top of it.
3. Write your own name on top of that.
4. What a mess!

EXAMPLE
1· Eleanor
2· Eleanor
3· Eleanor

When we make a mess of things, God helps us sort it out.

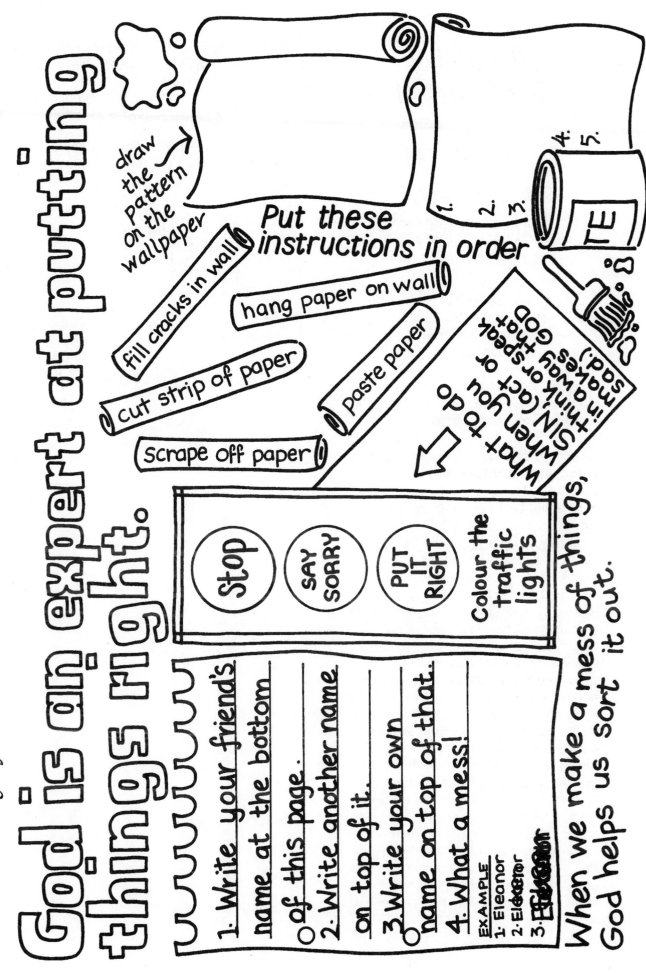

7th Sunday after Pentecost

YEAR 1

Thought for the day:
Since we are made in God's likeness,
the only real and fulfilling way to live
is in a loving, Godlike way.

Readings
Psalm 81
Genesis 50:15-end
1 John 2:1-17

Aim: To help the children look at choosing God's way of behaving.

Start by playing a quick game, such as crab football where you all move around like this:

Talk together about the way we keep having to make choices in a game, and we sometimes know we've made bad decisions and messed things up. That's also true in life. Have a joint telling of the Joseph story – the part where the brothers had decided to get rid of Joseph. So the brothers had really messed things up for Joseph. Or had they? Explain how God always works to bring some good out of our mistakes. Can they think of any good that came out of what the brothers had done? Make a list of these, then tell or read what happened when their father had

died, pausing to let them guess how Joseph will react to the brothers' story. (They may well recognise the temptation to twist the truth to get out of trouble!) Then go on to see what Joseph actually said.

Help them make this choosing chart and try it out on their friends and family.

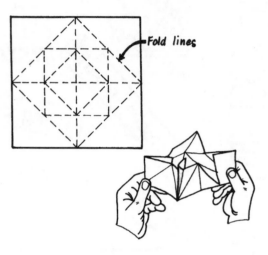

Fold lines

Living the loving way

MATCH THE SHAPES

cheer them up

help them if they put it

be friendly to them

make it up

if you have had a row

if they have lost something

if they are sad

if someone is lonely

This is what I want to do to make the world a better place _____

(Draw your ideas here)

Colour the coat

J	B	D	I	E	D
F	A	S	B	E	A
C	C	C	R	B	G
E	K	A	O	D	H
V	D	R	T	B	P
A	O	E	H	H	E
G	O	D	E	K	S
R	G	R	R	J	O
O	O	I	S	L	J
F	A	T	H	E	R

When Joseph's FATHER, JACOB, DIED, Joseph's BROTHERS were SCARED. They thought that JOSEPH would pay them BACK now. But Joseph FORGAVE them. "In all things," he said, "GOD works FOR GOOD."

7th Sunday after Pentecost

YEAR 2

Thought for the day:
We are to love others in the way God
loves us – completely.

Readings
Psalm 81
Deuteronomy 24:10-end
1 John 3:13-end

Aim: For the children to see that God's way is love in action.

Start by having a game of Simon Says, so that they make sure they only follow out the actions which Simon has told them to. Explain that in our lives we will probably hear all kinds of ideas about how to act, but if we listen carefully we'll be able to know which instructions come from God's will, and which don't. Give them some examples to practise on; if they think a suggestion comes from God they stand up – if not they stay sitting down. Some possible examples to start you making your own up:
Take that sweet – the shopkeeper isn't looking.
Give Mum a hand – she looks tired.
Wait for your friend to catch up.
Pretend you weren't involved in the fight.
Own up.
Then make some sweets or cakes, following the instructions. Hand them round afterwards on paper plates which have this written on them:
TRUE LOVE SHOWS IN ACTION.

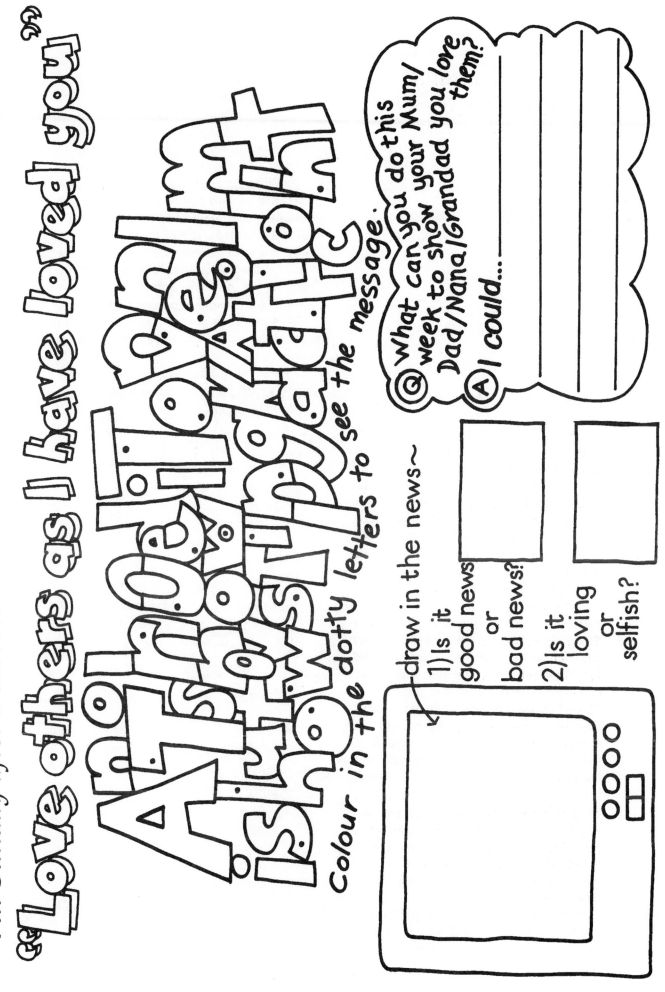

"Love others as I have loved you"

Colour in the dotty letters to see the message.

draw in the news~
1) Is it good news or bad news?

2) Is it loving or selfish?

Q) What can you do this week to show your Mum/Dad/Nana/Grandad you love them?

A) I could...

8th Sunday after Pentecost

YEAR 1

Thought for the day:
What we are determines how we fruit.

Readings
Psalm 73
Numbers 11:16-17,24-29
Acts 8:4-25

Aim: For the children to get to know the story of Simon the Magician.

Get the children in a huddle in the centre of the room to tell them about how the early church met together and worshipped in Jerusalem. Explain that people started to persecute the Christians, especially the Greek speaking ones, so they scattered away from Jerusalem to be safe. (Some children are sent off in different directions.) One of these people was a man called Philip, and he went to Samaria.

How do you think God brought good out of these persecutions? All the Christians who scattered, went and told people about Jesus wherever they went, so the good news spread and spread.

Now take everyone over to Samaria, to watch what Philip is up to. Let the children act out the story as you tell them how Philip was gathering groups and telling them about God's love for them, healing the sick and giving the blind their sight in Jesus's name. Many believed, and Philip baptised them in the rivers. Among those being baptised was a person called Simon, who was a clever magician and was very impressed with what Philip was doing.

Now the Christians at Jerusalem sent Peter and John to find out what was going on. (Have two people coming over from Jerusalem.) They were very pleased to find all these new Christians in the land which was the home of the Jews' traditional enemy, and they laid hands on them so they could receive the Holy Spirit. The new Christians started speaking in different tongues and dancing around full of the Spirit. Simon the magician wanted to buy this power, so he could do it to people and have control over them. The apostles were furious that he should think such a thing, and had to pray over Simon for him to be freed from wanting power all the time. God's power is always freely given, and can never be bought, either by money, or even by good deeds.

Help the children to express some part of this story in paints, crayons, collage or clay.

8th Sunday after Pentecost

Good trees make good fruit

THE SPIRIT'S GOOD FRUIT IN YOU

Yes / No

25p 8p

10p 5p

1. ✂ + ✏ =

2. ✏ + ✂ =

3. ✏ + ✂ =

What does it cost?

God's Power is always

1. Join the dots to see the picture.
2. Now add your own SVELAE and RIFUT.

8th Sunday after Pentecost

YEAR 2

Thought for the day:
What we are determines how we fruit.

Readings
Psalm 73
Proverbs 8:1-17
Luke 6:39-end

Aim: For the children to understand the sense of building their lives on Jesus.

Begin by talking about earthquakes, floods and have some pictures of what happens to houses that are built on a place where these things happen. Pray together for the people whose lives and property are destroyed or ruined in such disasters. Why do people live in such dangerous areas? Usually because they can't live anywhere else. There's no way anyone would choose to build in an unsafe place. Then explain how Jesus said that anyone who hears God's word and instead of following it, turns his back on it, is as barmy as this: someone actually choosing to build their house on sand, knowing that it won't survive the storms and floods.

Get the children to act out the story, with their bodies becoming the houses and the floods, and their voices the sound effects.

Give each child a small box to make into a house called 'Marion/Julian's Life' built on Jesus. They can use the box at home to keep treasures in.

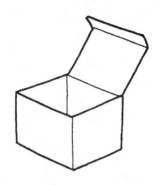

8th Sunday after Pentecost

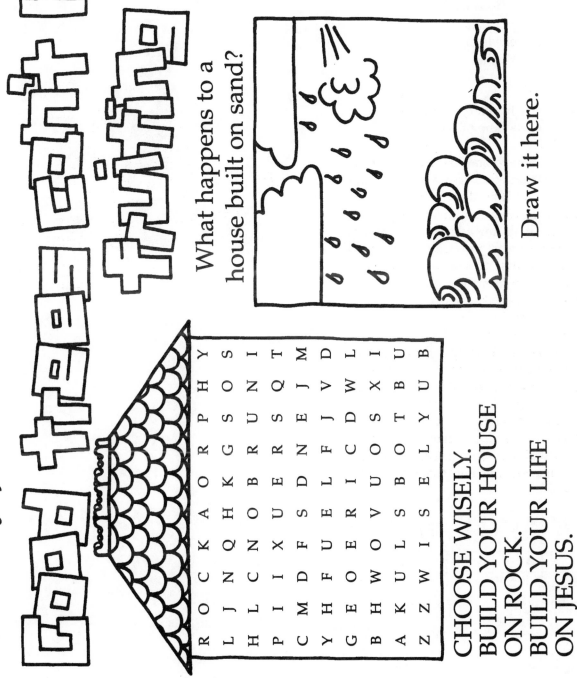

God trees can't help

New

Building truths

help

can't

people

good

living

Good

lives.

What happens to a house built on sand?

Draw it here.

```
R O C K A O R P H Y
L J N Q H K G S O S
H L C N O B R U N I
P I I X U E R S Q T
C M D F S D N E J M
Y H F U E L F J V D
G E O E R I C D W L
B H W O V U O S X I
A K U L S B O T B U
Z Z W I S E L Y U B
```

CHOOSE WISELY.
BUILD YOUR HOUSE
ON ROCK.
BUILD YOUR LIFE
ON JESUS.

9th Sunday after Pentecost

YEAR 1

Thought for the day:
God's protection against evil will
enable us to get on with his work.

Readings
Psalm 90
Nehemiah 4:7-end
Matthew 6:1-18

Aim: To hear the story of Nehemiah and the people rebuilding the city walls.

This is a good story to act out, with a group of children to be the builders, and others to be the scoffers and invaders. If you feel this may get too realistic with your group, go for a less direct telling, such as puppets, or using carpet tiles with cut outs of the builders and invaders. Bring out the important fact that all action was preceded by prayer, so that the whole plan was much more effective.

Then help them make this building game to play at home, so as to remind them. To play the game they will need a dice, and gradually the walls are rebuilt according to the numbers thrown. If a 6 is thrown, invaders are attacking at your part of the wall, and you must miss a turn while you cope with them.

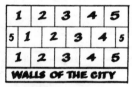

Enough for one per player

15 bricks of card per player

God's armour protects us.

How do you feel...

① when people tease you?
② when someone listens to you?

③ when someone likes you?
④ when people talk about you behind your back?
⑤ when people laugh at you?
⑥ when people cheer you on?

Here are the walls of the City of Jerusalem, Draw in 6 guards where you think you will most use them.

KEEP IN TOUCH WITH GOD, and he will help you.

9th Sunday after Pentecost

YEAR 2

Thought for the day:
God's protection against evil will
enable us to get on with his work.

Readings
Psalm 90
2 Samuel 1:1-12, 17-end
1 Timothy 6:6-end

Aim: To experience being prepared to do something.

Start by playing 'What's the secret?' You have a child at the front and give them items, one by one. The other children have to guess what the child is being prepared for.

For instance, Jane might be given a leotard, some grease paint, a script, a ghastly costume and some ballet shoes. Her secret: she's going to be in a show.

Alexander is given a lunch pack, a torch, a rucksack, a pair of thick socks, a map and a pair of boots. (Nothing needs to fit, as the children won't be dressing up.) Alexander's secret: He's going on a night hike.

Sam is given a bag of flour and a bowl, some cheese and a grater, a tin of tomatoes, an onion and some oven gloves. His secret: he's going to make a pizza.

Now explain to the children how God prepares us in our lives and equips us for what he need us to do. When Paul knew that his young friend Timothy was going to be a church worker, he wrote a letter full of advice. Read them a little of that letter, so they can hear it as a personal one. Have another child in the front to be Timothy. This time we work backwards – we already know what he is being prepared for; we're going to work out what he might need for the job.

If you have a blackboard or flip chart you can write or draw what they suggest, which will probably be extremely practical!

Safe to get on with God's work.

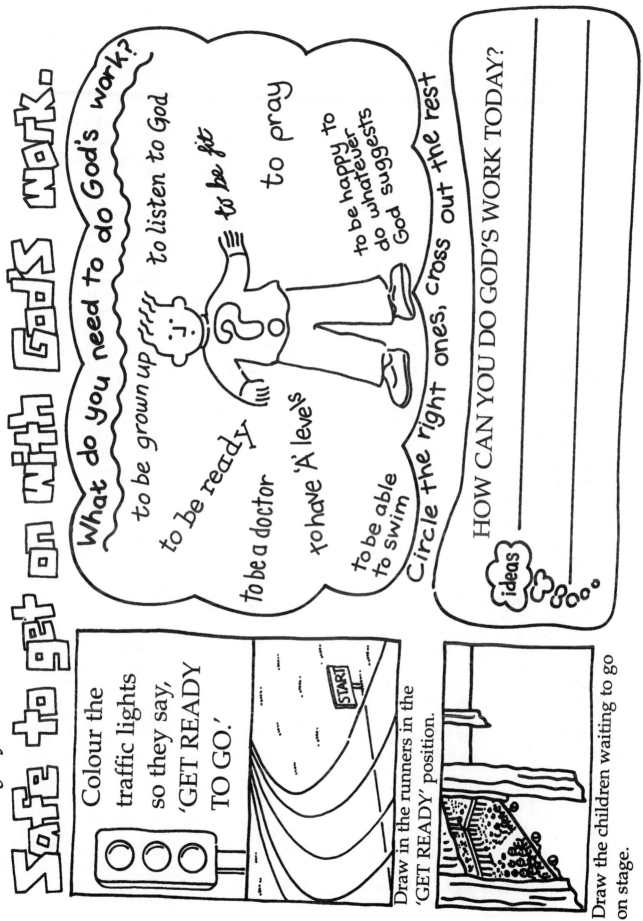

What do you need to do God's work?

to be grown up
to listen to God
to be fit
to pray
to be happy to do whatever God suggests
to be ready
to be a doctor
to have 'A' levels
to be able to swim

Circle the right ones, cross out the rest

Colour the traffic lights so they say, 'GET READY TO GO.'

START

Draw in the runners in the 'GET READY' position.

Draw the children waiting to go on stage.

HOW CAN YOU DO GOD'S WORK TODAY?

ideas

10th Sunday after Pentecost

YEAR 1

Thought for the day:
God's wisdom turns our priorities
upside down.

Readings
Psalm 19
1 Samuel 18:1-16
Mark 9:30-end

Aim: For the children to understand that God's nature is to be loving and merciful.

Have a selection of shapes for the children to handle and make patterns with. You can get sets of plastic or wooden shapes from Galt or The Early Learning Centre or you can make them as a resource from coloured card.

When the children have experienced the shapes, ask them to close their eyes, pick one up, guess what it is and then open their eyes to check if they were right, and let this lead on to what it is about a circle or square which makes them easy to tell apart. Can a circle ever be a square? Can a triangle ever be round? No. It's their nature to be the kind of shape they are.

What's God's nature? Jot up their ideas on a chart and keep asking 'How do you know?' Have some bibles and illustrated bible stories at hand to show God's nature being shown in action.

Now help the children to make this moving model. The qualities which come round into the mind bubble could be taken from what the children have just been talking about, or they can be these, which are like Jesus expressing his thoughts:

- we all need to love one another.
- don't be afraid – I am with you.
- trust me – I will never let you down.
- I will be with you always.
- I forgive you – go in peace.

10th Sunday after Pentecost

How does God think?
What is he like?

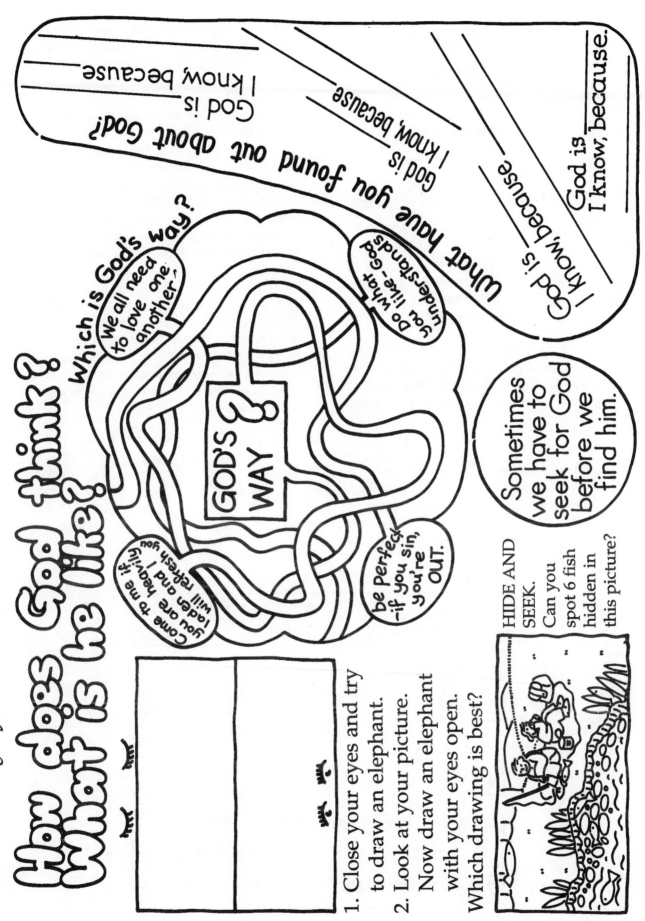

Which is God's way?

We all need to love one another.

Do what you like - God understands.

GOD'S WAY ?

Come th me if you are heavy laden and I will refresh you.

be Perfect - if you sin, you're OUT.

Sometimes we have to seek for God before we find him.

What have you found out about God?

God is _____
I know, because. _____

God is _____
I know, because. _____

God is _____
I know, because _____

God is _____
I know, because _____

1. Close your eyes and try to draw an elephant.
2. Look at your picture. Now draw an elephant with your eyes open. Which drawing is best?

HIDE AND SEEK. Can you spot 6 fish hidden in this picture?

10th Sunday after Pentecost

YEAR 2

Thought for the day:
God's wisdom turns our priorities
upside down.

Readings
Psalm 19
2 Samuel 9
Matthew 6:19-end

Aim: For the children to understand the way seeking God and his righteousness can free their lives from worry and strain.

Have one child walking around the circle looking more and more worried as the other children call out things to make him worried. (i.e. 'You're all on your own in the dark'; 'you've forgotten your swimming kit'; 'you're out shopping and suddenly realise everyone's gone home without you'.) Talk with the children about the things that worry them. This may lead into a time of prayer, and may also provide leaders with insights which will help them to pray more specifically for the children during the week.

Now look at what Jesus has to say about worrying. Either read the passage from Matthew, or tell it in your own words with the children acting out dressing and eating and so on, so that you can then go through the reading again in actions, which will help them remember it.

Now split the children into small groups to go on a treasure hunt. Each team is given a coded clue to start them off, and when they have solved it they go to the leader, who gives them the next clue to find from somewhere else. Eventually the clue words should make up the message:

STORE UP RICHES FOR YOURSELF
IN HEAVEN.

172

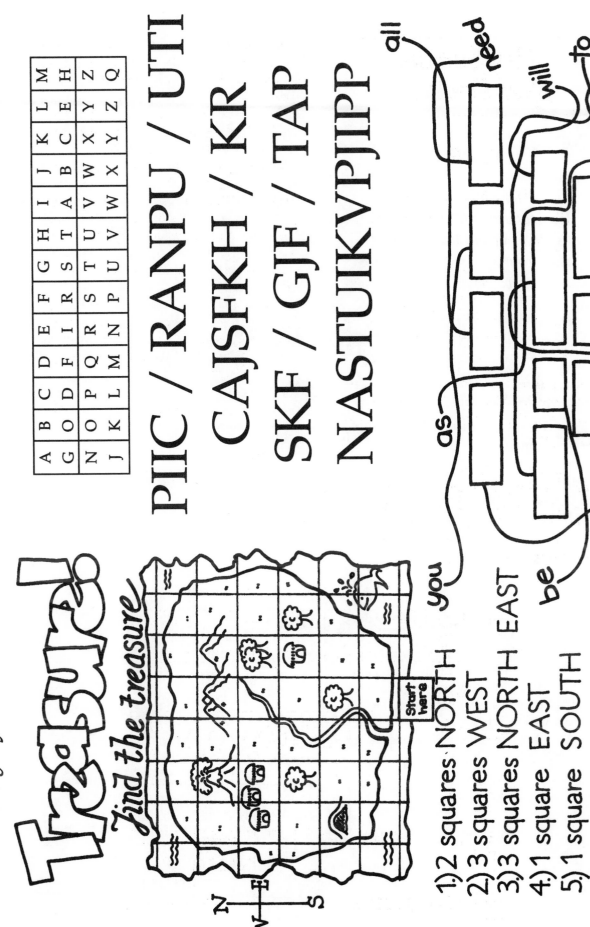

Treasure!
find the treasure

A	B	C	D	E	F	G	H	I	J	K	L	M
G	O	D	F	I	R	S	T	A	B	C	E	H
N	O	P	Q	R	S	T	U	V	W	X	Y	Z
J	K	L	M	N	P	U	V	W	X	Y	Z	Q

PIIC / RANPU / UTI

CAJSFKH / KR

SKF / GJF / TAP

NASTUKVPJIPP

1) 2 squares NORTH
2) 3 squares WEST
3) 3 squares NORTH EAST
4) 1 square EAST
5) 1 square SOUTH
The treasure is _____

Start here

N E S W

you   as   need   all   will   to   well   given   you   be   then

11th Sunday after Pentecost

YEAR 1

Thought for the day:
It's not God's will that we burn
ourselves out, but that we support
and encourage one another as we
serve those in need.

Readings
Psalms 123,124,125
Exodus 18:13-26
Acts 6

Aim: To think about how we can be a serving community.

Begin with an activity which can only work when everyone pulls together, such as parachute games, or creating a structure out of bodies (as in the Halifax building society advertisements). Then read or tell the events of Exodus 18, with the children acting it out. They can all do the queuing up for Moses and then make several queues once the other leaders have been chosen.

Talk together about how we can help people with their difficulties of housing, or not having fresh water, using atlases and aid organisation materials to anchor the discussion in reality.

Work together on creating posters for the event you plan to help.

11th Sunday after Pentecost

Many hands make light work

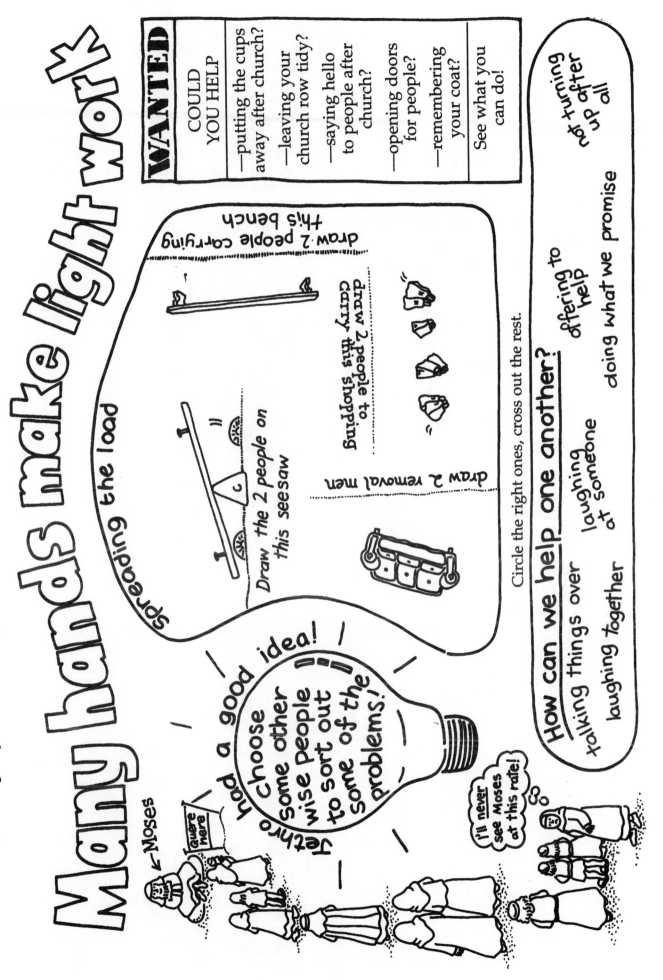

11th Sunday after Pentecost

YEAR 2

Thought for the day:
It's not God's will that we burden one another, but that we give one another encouragement and support.

Readings
Psalms 123,124,125
1 Kings 12:1-20
2 Corinthians 9

Aim: To help the children see that some things we do make life easier/harder for others.

Have a skipping rope and lay it across the floor and let everyone walk over it. Then lift it a little off the ground and everyone tries to cross, and gradually you make it wider and wider. The task gets harder and harder until no one can do it at all. Have an assistant offer to help the children over, and see how help makes all the difference. God wants us to make life easier for one another. Talk about ways they can do this.

Alternatively have a beanbag thrown round the group. If you don't catch it, you have to catch it next time with one hand, then on one leg, then kneeling on one knee, then kneeling on both knees. Each time you catch the ball you can work your way up to catching it standing up with both hands again.

Talk about how difficult it is when the game gets harder and harder, just when you need a bit of help. Life sometimes feels like that.

Talk together about some of the things that weigh them down and make life difficult, and then think of things that weigh other people down. Pray for these people. Now read the passage from 2 Corinthians 9 and think of ways the children could help some of the people they have been praying for. Plan what to do and start working towards it.

11th Sunday after Pentecost

Helping one another along.

With our God it's possible...

1 TON

Who does each parcel belong to?

What things weigh people down?

Choose one from the list and write it in the weight.
- SADNESS   - MONEY WORRIES
- LONELINESS   - FAMILY ROWS

How could you help,
when someone falls over? ....
when Mum's in a hurry? ....

12th Sunday after Pentecost

YEAR 1

Thought for the day:
It is both our privilege and our
responsibility to spread the good news
wherever we are put.

Readings
Psalms 145,150
Ezekiel 33:1-9,30-end
Acts 16:1-15

Aim: For the children to know the urgency of spreading the good news of God's love.

Beforehand prepare some letters, cards and bills in envelopes, some of which bring bad, unwelcome news, and some which bring good, encouraging news. Put them in a bag, and have one of the children as postman, delivering the post. As each item is delivered, it is opened up and read out. Everyone can make a suitable groan or thumbs up sign according to the news it brings.

Explain how some bad news is necessary, even if we don't like it, because it can help us put things right. Read or tell the events from Acts 16, where Paul, Timothy and Luke travel around wherever they feel God wants them to go, in order to bring people the good news of God's love which they know can fill their lives with colour and joy.

What kind of message would we like people to know about Jesus? Work on writing (or scribing) the messages, and illustrating them, before putting them in envelopes and sending them off to someone they know.

12th Sunday after Pentecost

Be brave—Speak OUT!

I would like everyone to know that God...

What nice things about God would you like people to know? Write or draw them here.

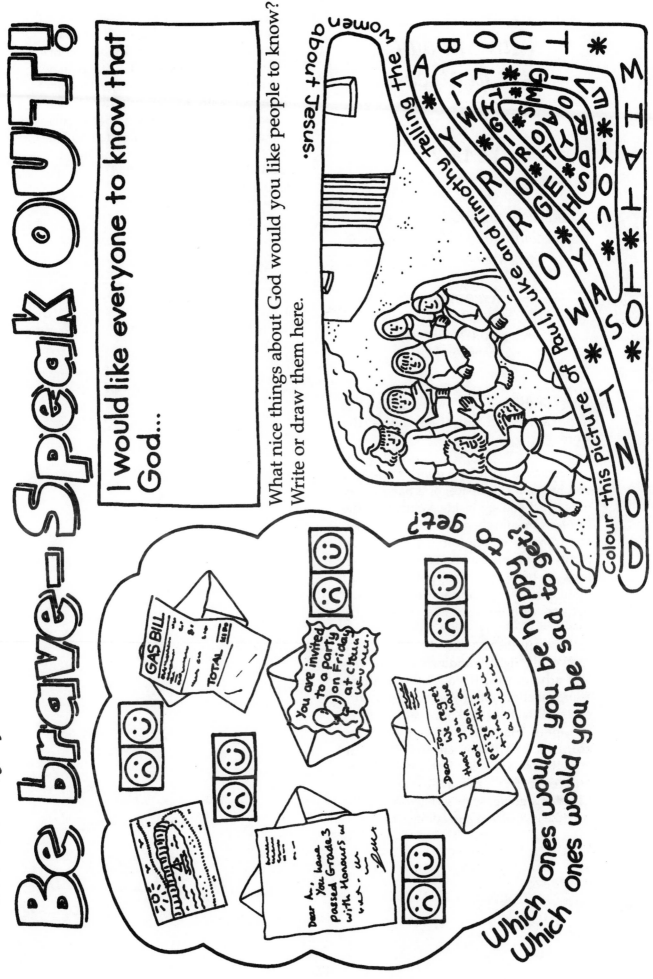

Colour this picture of Paul, Luke and Timothy telling the women about Jesus.

Which ones would you be sad to get?
Which ones would you be happy to get?

12th Sunday after Pentecost

YEAR 2

Thought for the day:
It is both our privilege and our
responsibility to spread the good news
wherever we are put.

Readings
Psalms 145,150
Amos 5:14-24 (or 6-24)
Romans 15:14-29

Aim: For the children to understand the importance and fun of spreading the word.

Prepare a paddling pool of water if you have outside space, or a baking tray of water if you are inside. Watch how the ripples spread right out to the edge when we drop something into the centre. Let plenty of people have a go at this. Then look at how ink, dropped onto wet blotting paper spreads and makes lovely patterns as it does so. Everyone can try this.

Now tell the children about Paul, in a 'cricket highlights' rundown of his travels and adventures. If you draw a rough approximation of the Mediterranean with chalk on the floor, and have card labels of the main place names, two or three children can move around it as the adventures are told. Put a card down wherever Paul got a new group of Christians going, so everyone can see the way the gospel was spreading.

Now give each child a small jar and a label on which they write 'DON'T KEEP THE FAITH – SPREAD IT!' When they have stuck their label on their jar, let them fill the jar with an individually chosen spread from an assortment of ingredients, such as raisins, honey, jam and chocolate chips. They can take these home and follow the instructions on their jar in the coming weeks.

12th Sunday after Pentecost

If we don't tell, they won't know

"You played really well"

"Catch hold of this!"

"Cheer up - I'll help you mend it"

"I hope you feel better soon"

Who is saying what?

How did you find out about Jesus?

☐ Someone told me

☐ I read about him

DID YOU KNOW

There are still lots of people who don't know that Jesus is REAL and ALIVE.

Where did you get to know Jesus?

☐ at home

☐ at school

☐ at church

☐ at holiday club

☐ at my friend's house

How can we let them know? IDEAS

_____

_____

_____

_____

_____

1. Think of a person you know who doesn't think Jesus is real.

2. Write their name here ....

3. Pray for them at least once EVERY DAY until you are 18.

"Dear Jesus, I would love .... to know you are real and that you love them very much. Amen"

13th Sunday after Pentecost

YEAR 1

Thought for the day:
Being a Christian doesn't take all the suffering away, but transforms our way of dealing with it.

Readings
Psalms 130,137:1-6
2 Kings 19:8-19
Acts 16:16-end

Aim: To introduce the children to the story of Paul and Silas in prison.

Have a few ball and chains made from card circles and paper chains made with black or shiny paper. Prison bars can be oven shelves, held up in front of the prisoners.

Begin by sharing memories of some of the worst times in their lives, and how they felt during those times. Then tell or read the story of Paul and Silas, with the children making the appropriate sounds for the whipping, and the doors clanging shut. Have some of the children fastened up with the ball and chains, and then think how Paul and Silas must have felt. Yet they sang! (They can sing their favourite songs at this point.) Have some children using instruments such as shakers, drums and cymbals to create the earthquake, and call out above the noise, as Paul did, so that the children can sense the panic and confusion with Paul in control.

After the story (which the children may well want to do twice, to get it really lifelike) talk about how we can sing our praises in those worst times, knowing that God is good, even if we are in a sticky patch, and giving God praise in those times is one of the best presents we can give him.

Have a time of prayer for all those who are in prison for believing in God at the moment, and help the children make these balls and chains to take home.

How it helps to be a Christian

What do you do when things go wrong?

a) SULK
b) GRUMBLE AT EVERYONE
c) PUT UP WITH IT

I know it sounds crazy, but if we praise God in the bad times, he can bring some good out of them, and you will feel better.

So....

When you lose your purse...

When your best team loses ...

When no-one understands you...

When anything goes wrong ...

Colour this picture of Paul and Silas in prison, singing cheerfully to God

How many words can you get out of 'PRISON PRAISE'

13th Sunday after Pentecost

YEAR 2

Thought for the day:
Being a Christian doesn't take all the
suffering away, but transforms our
way of dealing with it.

Readings
Psalms 130,137:1-6
Isaiah 49:13-23
Matthew 11:20-end

Aim: For the children to know that Jesus knows us by name and can really help us if we let him.

Start by providing strips of material or scarves for the children to try walking about three-legged with a partner. This doesn't have to be a competitive race – it's really the experience of learning to walk 'yoked up' to someone else that is important.

Now show the children some pictures from the library history books of oxen yoked up together, and explain how the farmers would put a young, inexperienced animal yoked to a strong, experienced ox, so that the young one would learn how to work and the load wouldn't be so hard to pull. Talk together about their three-legged walks. They will probably have noticed how difficult it was at first with both pulling different ways, and how much easier it was once they had learnt to walk exactly in step with each other.

Now read the part from Matthew about Jesus' invitation to all the weary and heavily burdened. Why will it help to be yoked up with Jesus? Pray together for those who don't yet know they can let Jesus take the strain in their lives, and for all who carry burdens of some kind.

Then help the children to make this model of oxen yoked together.

God never forgets you—let him help you.

How good is your memory?

Shopping List

bread
4 yoghurts
tin of tomatoes
onions
crisps
jam

1. Read the list carefully.

2. Turn over and write them down or draw all you remember.

3. Check with the list.
HOW MANY DID YOU REMEMBER?

God's memory is

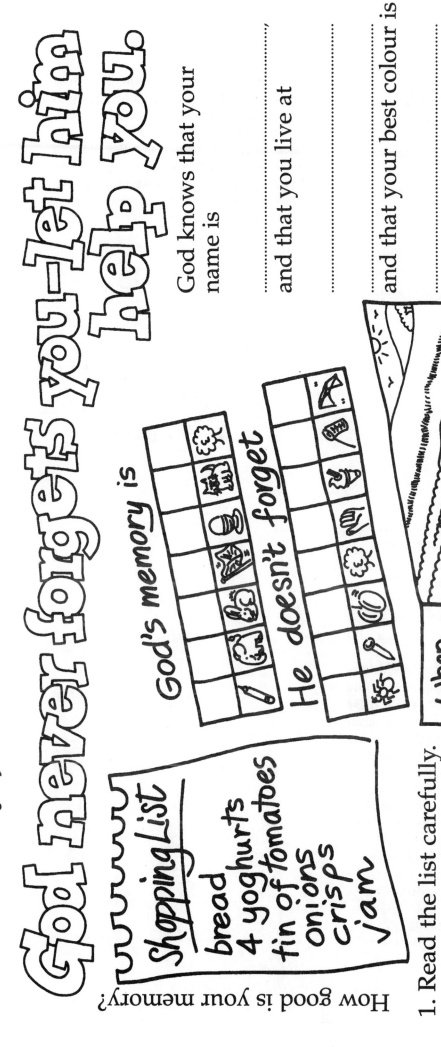

He doesn't forget

God knows that your name is
....

and that you live at
....

and that your best colour is
....

God knows you very well, and he loves you!

When we join Jesus he can help us, too.

Colour this picture of oxen yoked together.

14th Sunday after Pentecost

YEAR 1

Thought for the day:
Whatever our age or marital status,
we are all children in God's family,
brothers and sisters bound together
by love.

Readings
Psalm 103
Genesis 29:1-20
2 Timothy 1:1-14

Aim: For the children to feel part of God's family.

Begin with the animal family game. Everyone is told in a whisper what type of animal they are, and whether they are the Mum, Dad or Baby of that animal. Then everyone makes their animal noise, trying to meet up with the rest of the family. When they are ready, Dad stands behind a chair, Mum sits on the chair, and Baby sits on Mum's lap.

Now talk together about the things they like doing at home with their family – the people they live with. Write these up on a sheet of paper. Then talk about the things they don't enjoy and write these up on another sheet. It is important that the children accept that no home life is perfect; sometimes children think theirs is the only home where people shout at each other, and are quite relieved to find it's quite a normal part of family life for people to get cross with one another sometimes. In the discussion, talk about ways of making up and putting things right, and if children don't want to contribute, don't draw attention to this.

Let the children pick something from each list to draw, and stick the pictures on to the inside and outside of a paper plate. Round the rim write GOD'S LOVE . . . GOD'S LOVE . . . GOD'S LOVE . . . on both sides, so that they know that their own human family is held in the love of God, both at the good and the difficult times.

Paper plate

186

14th Sunday after Pentecost

All God's sons and daughters

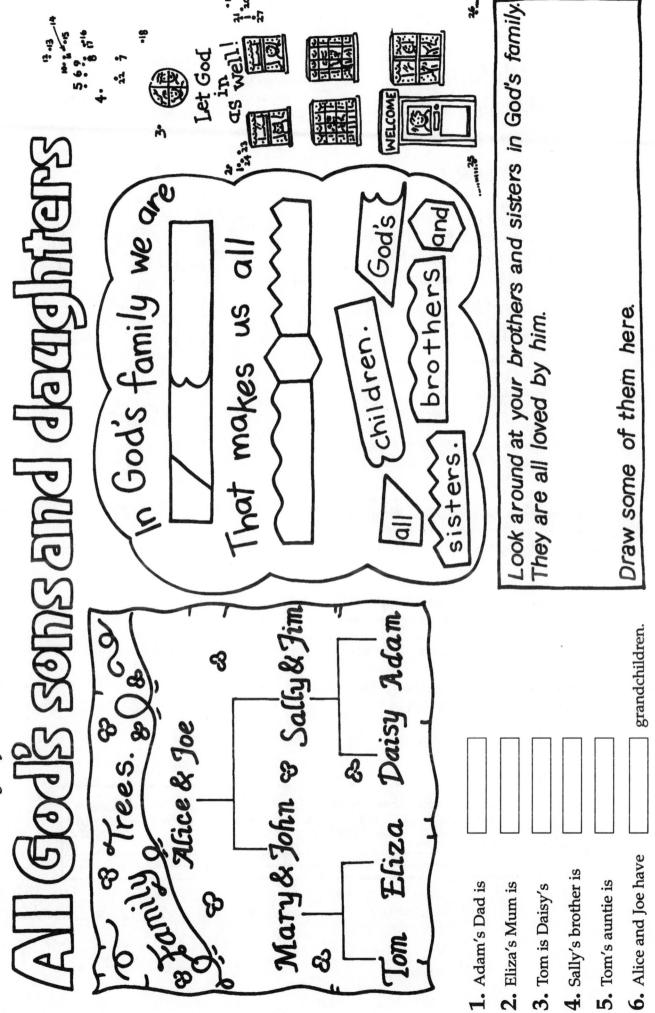

Family 8 Trees. 8

8 Alice & Joe

Mary & John & Sally & Jim

Tom Eliza Daisy Adam

In God's family we are

That makes us all

God's

children.

all

sisters.

brothers and

Let God in as well!

WELCOME

Look around at your brothers and sisters in God's family. They are all loved by him.

Draw some of them here.

1. Adam's Dad is

2. Eliza's Mum is

3. Tom is Daisy's

4. Sally's brother is

5. Tom's auntie is

6. Alice and Joe have _____ grandchildren.

14th Sunday after Pentecost

YEAR 2

Thought for the day:
Whatever our age or marital status,
we are all children in God's family,
brothers and sisters bound together
by love.

Readings
Psalm 103
Genesis 47:1-12
Colossians 3:12-21

Aim: To see the settling of Jacob's family in Egypt as part of the whole bible story.

Have a timeline drawn on a long strip of paper (see below) and fill in the main characters and events on it as you go on a whistle stop tour through to Joseph and his brothers. The children may be able to help you, filling in details of individual stories as you go. When you get to Joseph, slow the pace and increase the detail, getting the children to join in the acting out of the story, or using the 'carpet tiles' method of story telling. Make sure the children are aware of the change of place, and the geography of it.

Then make a communal model of the whole family plus animals in Goshen, using upturned bowls and plates under a large cloth to make hills and valleys, pipe cleaners and cloth for people and paper cut-out sheep.

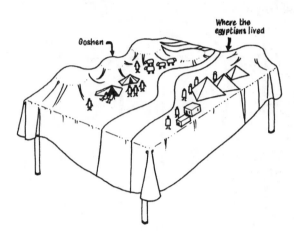

God calls Abraham	Isaac born	Jacob and Esau born	Esau sells his birthright	Jacob marries Leah and Rachel		Joseph born	Joseph sold to Egypt

14th Sunday after Pentecost

We are all in God's family

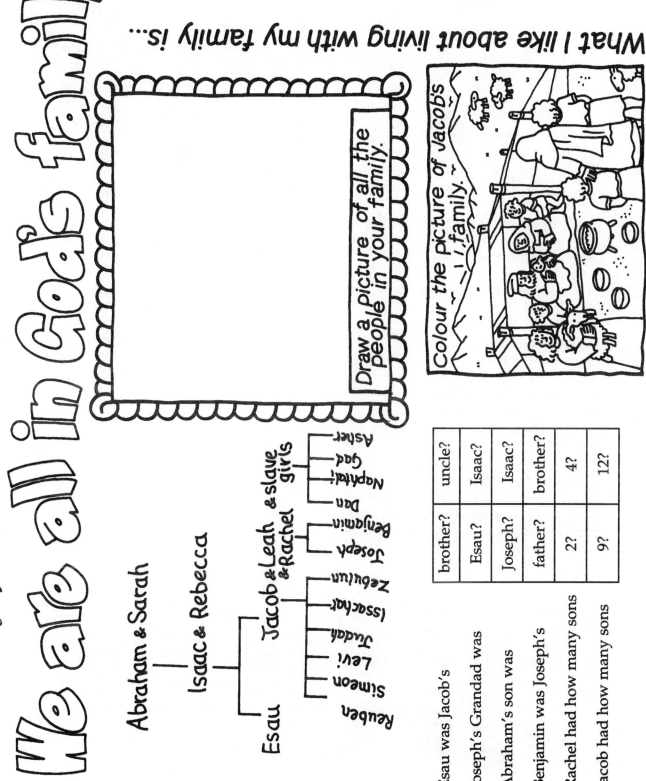

Abraham & Sarah

Isaac & Rebecca

Esau   Jacob & Leah & slave
              & Rachel   girls

Reuben
Simeon
Levi
Judah
Issachar
Zebulun

Joseph
Benjamin

Dan
Naphtali
Gad
Asher

Draw a picture of all the people in your family.

What I like about living with my family is...

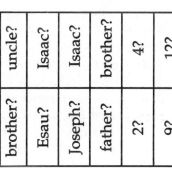

Colour the picture of Jacob's family.

1. Esau was Jacob's	brother?	uncle?
2. Joseph's Grandad was	Esau?	Isaac?
3. Abraham's son was	Joseph?	Isaac?
4. Benjamin was Joseph's	father?	brother?
5. Rachel had how many sons	2?	4?
6. Jacob had how many sons	9?	12?

15th Sunday after Pentecost

YEAR 1

Thought for the day:
God is the One who has power over our lives and everything we do.

Readings
Psalm 50
Daniel 5
Acts 25:1-12

Aim: For the children to see how Paul's reaction to his hardships showed that Jesus was Lord of his life.

First play the 'Simon says' game, in which they have to listen out for the authority of 'Simon' before carrying out the orders.

If possible have a man to tell Paul's story from Paul's point of view, putting on the appropriate headgear to do so. If you have no men on the team, try to borrow someone for the morning. Whoever does the telling will need to prepare the story from Acts 20, when Paul goes to Jerusalem and the Jews attack him. The children can be brought into the story as the Pharisees and the Sadducees. Have a question time afterwards, with the children questioning Paul (still in character) about his adventures.

Point out that what made the Jews so angry was that Paul was saying Jesus was Lord – that a human was God. It is an amazing thing to claim, but it's true. Go over the things Jesus did which make it clear that Jesus really is the Christ everyone had been waiting for, and try this simple creed. The responses need to be really loud.

Who was there before anything else?
GOD WAS!

Who created the entire universe?
GOD DID!

Who is in charge of our universe today?
GOD IS!

Who was walking this earth as Jesus?
GOD WAS!

Who loves us so much that he died
for us all?
GOD DOES!

Who is alive for ever and living in
his people?
GOD IS!

Who do we believe in?
WE BELIEVE IN GOD!

Help the children to make some bracelets, anklets and neck bands to wear. (See bottom of page.)

15th Sunday after Pentecost

God is the one with real power.

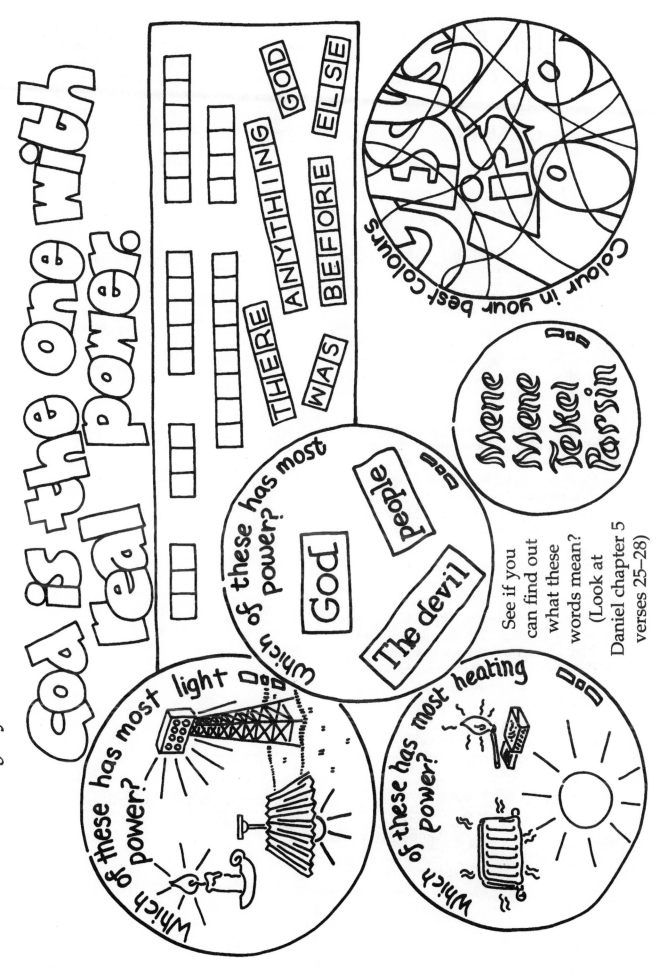

THERE ANYTHING GOD

WAS BEFORE ELSE

Colour in your best colours

Jesus

Mene Mene Tekel Parsin

Which of these has most power?

God

people

The devil

See if you can find out what these words mean? (Look at Daniel chapter 5 verses 25–28)

Which of these has most light power?

Which of these has most heating power?

15th Sunday after Pentecost

YEAR 2

Thought for the day:
God is the One who has power over our lives and everything we do.

Readings
Psalm 50
1 Samuel 8:4-22a
1 Peter 2:11-end

Aim: For the children to learn about obedience to God, and to those who look after us.

Have everyone moving round the room in the ways you direct – forwards, backwards, sideways, slowly, quickly etc. From time to time tell them to stop and then go again. Talk about obeying orders and making an effort to do this without arguing! Talk about how difficult it is to obey when you really want to do something else instead, and suggest ways to improve this for everyone. (Asking for it to be made known before the final deadline for finishing a game and going to bed; having a family rota for house jobs, so that everyone agrees what is fair; deciding in advance on bedtimes, getting up times and hair wash days.)

Listen to what Peter has to say, and pray together for our own world leaders. Then everyone can help make a large painting of all kinds of different places we come across in our lives. Over each is stamped or stuck a JESUS IS LORD (see below).

God is in charge

Think of yourself as a place. Draw in flags where God is in charge.

JESUS rules OK

what I want
at school
with friends
my fears
what I say
at home
my temper
at swimming

What rules are needed where?

share with one another

walk in the corridors

stop talking and listen when you are asked to.

don't cheat

14,6,4,10   15,11,13   8,11,16,4   5,11,3

15,11,13   14,1,10,12   12,11   11,2,4,15   6,7,9

1,10,3   3,11   14,6,1,12   6,4   14,1,10,12,17.

A	B	D	E	G	H	I	L	M	N	O	T	U	W	Y	V	S
1	2	3	4	5	6	7	8	9	10	11	12	13	14	15	16	17

16th Sunday after Pentecost

YEAR 1

Thought for the day:
Treat others as you want them to treat you.

Readings
Psalm 107:1-32
1 Kings 21 (or 1-23)
Matthew 7:1-12

Aim: To hear the 'bad neighbour' story and look at Jesus' teaching on how to live peaceably with others.

Begin by playing games of 'piggy in the middle', using beanbags. This is actually an excellent example of how the problem of being left out and then spoiling a game has been solved by it being made into a game.

Now tell the story of Naboth's vineyard. You could do this effectively by having it told three times from different viewpoints – first the king's, then the queen's, then Naboth's. Or you could have pictures of the main characters and display them on the floor, or on an OHP whenever they come into the story. Or you could have the children acting it out as you do the narrative, with everyone joining in the crowd scenes. Whichever way you do it, bring out the underhand and cruel way Naboth was dealt with, and after the story talk with the children about what a bad and unjust thing it was to do. What do they think Ahab should have done? And suppose he had still gone all sulky, what do they think Jezebel should have done?

Now look at what Jesus said we should do – treat others as you would want them to treat you. See if they can learn this off by heart by singing it over and over again to the tune of 'Twinkle, twinkle little star'. It fits in squashily, so long as you make 'treat others' fit with 'twinkle' like this:

Twin-kle,	twin-kle,
Treat oth-ers as	you would-want

lit-tle	star
them to-treat	you

It makes a tongue twister!

16th Sunday after Pentecost

Treat others as you want them to treat you.

King AHAB and Queen JEZEBEL lived next door to their NEIGHBOUR. His name was NABOTH and he owned a VINE-YARD. Ahab wanted it and asked to BUY it but Naboth said NO. Ahab began to SULK. Jezebel sorted it out by having Naboth MURDERED.

```
J E Z E B E L S D T
N B H J A U D E S R
S A C G B L R B U Y
D T B P K E A O L T
I C N O D C B I K O
S E Q R T H D M A P
A R U F G H J F N Y
H M V I N E Y A R D
A U E V H X Z D F Z
B N W E U S G H U G
```

What are we very good at being, without having to practise?

Colour the dotty letters to find out.

ASK and you will _____

Seek and you will _____

Knock and the door _____

find

will be opened

receive

Award for being the WORST NEIGHBOURS OF THE YEAR goes to
A.............. and J..............

Do 🔑 they 👏 🔑

g⊘+dge g⊘pw g⊘+dge i.

16th Sunday after Pentecost

YEAR 2

Thought for the day:
Treat others as you want them to treat you.

Readings
Psalm 107:1-32
Proverbs 25:6-22
James 2:1-13

Aim: For the children to understand the teaching of James and to look at our own behaviour in the light of it.

First have a game where one end of the room is 'Being a good neighbour', the other end is 'Being a bad neighbour' and the middle is 'Names of people who are our neighbours'. As you call out something from the categories, everyone runs to the appropriate position. Good neighbour qualities may include such things as taking turns in a game, sometimes playing the game their friends want to play, helping at home without arguing, and making a get well card for someone in hospital. Bad neighbour qualities may include sulking if you don't get your own way, moaning about having to tidy your room, cheating at a game, and getting someone else into trouble when it's really your fault.

Names of neighbours may include the names of people in the parish (including some of the children's names), those they live with, share a table with at school, teachers they like and dislike, and friends and relations.

Then read the passage from Proverbs, using different voices for the various sayings, and act out together the teaching in James, so that they can see what ought to be done as well.

Finally help the children to make this circle of people joined in God's love, which could be taken home to use as a table centrepiece, putting a candle in the middle.

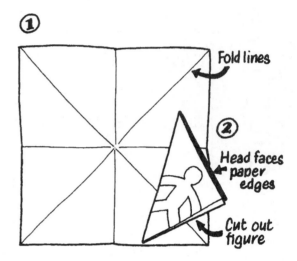

196

Love and respect each other.

If your enemy is thirsty...

give him a drink

give him an empty glass

pretend you have not noticed

Is there anyone new in church today? Make them feel

✳ = ▽ ▽ = C
▽ = E ⬚ = L
· = M ○ = ✳
△ = C □ = L
▷ = M

Colour this picture of some families coming in to church.

17th Sunday after Pentecost

YEAR 1

Thought for the day:
Work for God's glory, not your own.

Readings
Psalms 91, 93
Judges 7:1-8,19-23
John 7:1-24

Aim: For the children to understand the truth behind the Gideon story – faith shows in action; God knows what he's doing.

Begin with a sorting out game, such as all those wearing yellow run to the back wall; all those who ate cornflakes for breakfast hop to the centre; all who watch Superman leap across to the front wall etc.

Now tell the story of how God sorted out the soldiers and by following God closely, Gideon led his army to a rather clever victory. During the telling, hold a large version of the card the children will be making later, and break open the seal at the appropriate moment to reveal the light inside. We have a nativity play 'shepherds' fire' which also comes in handy at different times of the year; if you have one hidden away, bring it out and use it for when Gideon creeps down to hear what the enemy are saying. These few props really focus attention, making the storytelling very realistic.

Then help the children to make this card model of the hidden lights. As you all work on the models, talk informally about how we need to keep looking and listening to God, so that we notice what he is trying to tell us. You may be able to share a personal example of this so that the children understand that it really happens now.

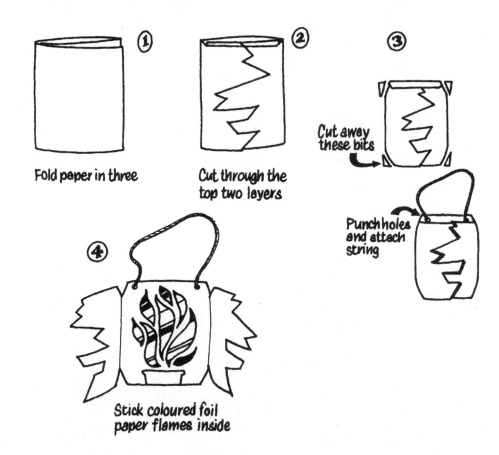

① Fold paper in three

② Cut through the top two layers

③ Cut away these bits
Punch holes and attach string

④ Stick coloured foil paper flames inside

Work for God's glory, not your own

If God is to work in us we need to

① [ ][ ][ ][ ][ ][ ]
② [ ][ ][ ][ ][ ]
③ [ ][ ][ ][ ][ ]

and

Colour this picture of Gideon and his soldiers breaking their clay pots.

match the words up

TORCHES   YLCA   ATSR

SCOTRHE

SOLDIERS

DIGNEO

CLAY JARS

GIDEON   DOSLIRES

17th Sunday after Pentecost

the walls of Jericho, so that when the army give their huge shout the walls can fall down.

YEAR 2

Thought for the day:
Work for God's glory, not your own.

Readings
Psalms 91, 93
Joshua 5:13-6:20
John 6:51-69

Aim: To help the children listen to God.

Begin by playing the 'keys' game, where everyone sits in a circle and one person sits blindfolded in the middle. Someone creeps round the outside of the circle, holding the keys, and the person in the middle has to listen for where they are. If they point directly to them, someone else can go in the middle.

Then have a time of quietness, listening to the sounds, and praying through them. Explain that Joshua, in today's story, listened to God and carried out his instructions, even though they were very strange instructions indeed.

Tell the story from a soldier's point of view, and have children standing up as

Afterwards, help the children make these trumpets.

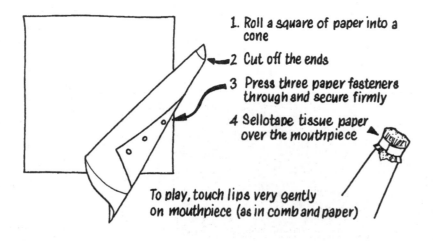

1. Roll a square of paper into a cone
2. Cut off the ends
3. Press three paper fasteners through and secure firmly
4. Sellotape tissue paper over the mouthpiece

To play, touch lips very gently on mouthpiece (as in comb and paper)

Not my will but God's will.

1.

2.

Colour this picture of the people marching around the city of Jericho. WHAT HAPPENED NEXT?

Draw it here.

```
J F E L L T N P
E O M E L I F O
R A S I D M T G
I J B H Q E U N
C I T Y U S O E
H K M C H A H V
O I W A L L S E
T R U M P E T S
```

JOSHUA told them to walk around the CITY of JERICHO SEVEN TIMES blowing their TRUMPETS. Then they gave a huge SHOUT and the WALLS FELL down.

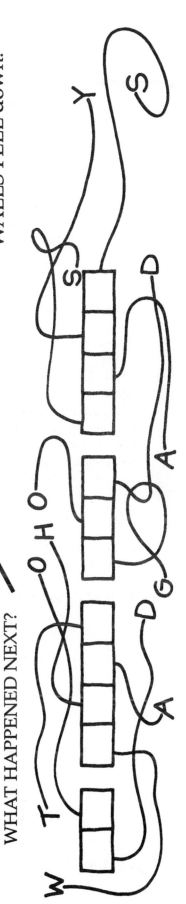

18th Sunday after Pentecost

YEAR 1

Thought for the day:
Live every day of your life to the full.

Readings
Psalm 118
Ecclesiastes 11 and 12
Luke 12:1-21

Aim: For the children to appreciate the lasting things and see the way other things don't last.

Start with blowing bubbles and enjoying them, noticing how we don't get terribly upset when they burst because we know that bubbles aren't built to last, and we don't expect anything more from them. If we did, we'd get very disappointed every time one popped.

Explain how sometimes people set their hearts on things they think will last – like money and power. How long do these things last? Only to death, at the very most.

Now tell the story from Luke, introducing it as it is in the bible – coming straight after two brothers wanting Jesus to sort out their squabble. (You may well have a couple of real squabbling brothers who would be happy to explain this part.)

During the telling of the story introduce some sound effects of the old barns being pulled down and the new ones built. Either have these previously taped, or have them being made by the children.

Then help them to make the three dimensional picture (shown below), which you can either look at or through, just as we can either fix our attention on this world and get disappointed, or we can look deeper into it and find real, lasting meaning.

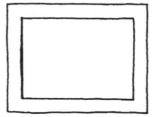

1 Make a card frame

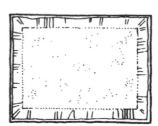

2 Stick coloured tissue paper on to the frame

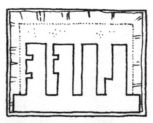

3 Cut out card shapes and stick on the back of frame

4 Look down at the picture and it is just a nice colour. Look up to the light and see LIFE

202

What things do you
like doing? Write
them here and thank
God for them.

18th Sunday after Pentecost

Live to the full!

Jesus says:

a t øu

GO+d

couldn't
g u h n't

f th

W
f

øa ru
h/lp

2

5.

1)How many feet
have you got? ☐
2)How many
fingers? ☐ ☐
3)How many nails? ☐
4)How many hairs on
your head? ☐

(Bet you couldn't do the last
question!)

Some things we can do.
Some things we can't do,
and never will be able to.

But God loves you
and ⬭ ☐.

you look will after ☐

18th Sunday after Pentecost

YEAR 2

Thought for the day:
Live every day of your life to the full.

Readings
Psalm 118
Jeremiah 26:1-16
Philippians 1:12-26

Aim: To help the children understand about living to the full in Christ.

Begin in a lively praise and worship time, with a real sense of celebration. Explain that although we could all think of lots of reasons for not celebrating, we're going to celebrate the sheer perfection of God loving us, and the fact that he can bring good out of every situation, however bad or terrible.

Tell the story of Jeremiah, and get them all to close round you, in a hostile, threatening way, before the officials give their verdict. Show the children how Jeremiah wasn't too bothered about their threats – he was far more bothered that they took some notice of his warnings, and got themselves right with God again. Have a bowl of water labelled LIFE, and using a Sindy and an Action man, dressed suitably, show how lots of people only dip their toes in life, never letting themselves go or getting deeply involved. As Christians, we are called to live life fully, getting ourselves totally immersed in it, and enjoying all the good things God gives us. That means an exciting life is in store for all who decide to follow Jesus – you just never know where or how you will be used next!

Help the children make these sliders which transform a very dull life into a very colourful one.

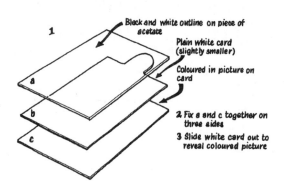

1

Black and white outline on piece of acetate

Plain white card (slightly smaller)

Coloured in picture on card

a

b

c

2. Fix a and c together on three sides

3 Slide white card out to reveal coloured picture

18th Sunday after Pentecost

How to be free – even in Prison.

What have you got to be happy about?

1. _____
2. _____
3. _____
4. _____
5. _____
6. _____
7. _____

See if you can think of 7 reasons for being happy.

The best place for me!

Circle the things that can stop you being free.

Birthdays

PRISON

WORRY

Pets

Chains

friends

Draw and colour the best place in the world you have been to. As you draw, thank God for the happy time you had there.

b=black
bl=blue
r=red
g=green
y=yellow

19th Sunday after Pentecost

YEAR 1

Thought for the day:
Commit your ways to God; he promises to look after your needs and he will not let you down.

Readings
Psalm 37:1-22
Job 23:1-12
2 Corinthians 1:1-22

Aim: For the children to deepen their understanding of what faith means.

Beforehand set up a length of wool around the room, or outside on a trail. First of all send people off in pairs to walk the trail. One of the pair is blindfold and holds on to the wool for guidance; the other person is there to encourage and direct, but not touch, unless really necessary. They then swap round. This is an excellent exercise for noticing how vulnerable we feel when we can't see and don't know where we are going.

When everyone has had a go, talk together about how they felt and what scared them. In our faith we can't always see very clearly, and have to feel our way through life bit by bit. But God has promised that those who seek will find, and he will always be there helping and guiding us and encouraging us as we go.

Then help the children to make a sign which says JESUS IS LORD, which they can even read with their eyes shut, because the letters are cut out of different materials.

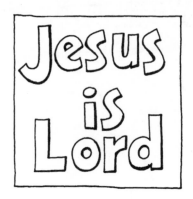

19th Sunday after Pentecost

God is real, even when we can't feel him there.

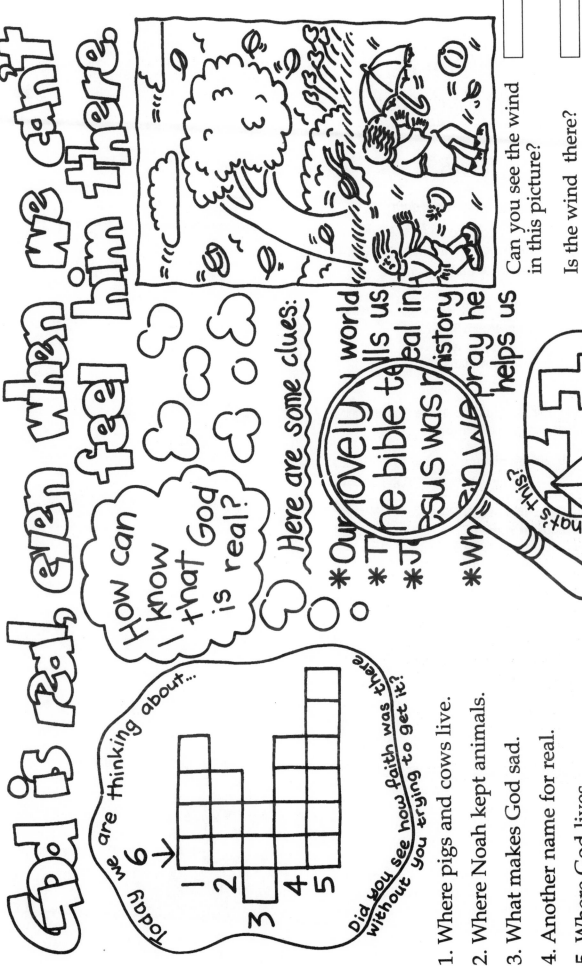

Today we are thinking about...

How can I know that God is real?

Here are some clues:

* Our lovely world
* The bible tells us
* Jesus was real in history
* When we pray he helps us

What's this?

9 o'clock!

Can you see the wind in this picture?

Is the wind there?

GOD IS THERE, EVEN THOUGH WE CAN'T SEE HIM.

Did you see how faith was there without you trying to get it?

1. Where pigs and cows live.
2. Where Noah kept animals.
3. What makes God sad.
4. Another name for real.
5. Where God lives.
6. Trusting God and believing in him.

19th Sunday after Pentecost

YEAR 2

Thought for the day:
Commit your ways to God; he
promises to look after your needs and
he will not let you down.

Readings
Psalm 37:1-22
Joshua 23
2 Corinthians 11:16-31

Aim: For the children to see that life as a Christian is an adventure.

Begin by playing a game like 'block', where everyone has to try and get back to a prearranged place without being caught by the keeper of this place.

Look at some of the adventures Paul had, just because he set out to tell people about Jesus. Have them written on different sheets of paper, and spread the children around them so that all the pictures are drawn and painted, or expressed in modelling clay or collage. The whole lot becomes an exhibition which can be spread around the room, so that everyone can walk through it, finishing with prayer.

You will need one or more pictures of Paul being beaten and left for dead, being beaten with rods, and being whipped. One of him being stoned, several of him being shipwrecked and one of drifting out to sea. You will need pictures of swollen rivers, Paul being attacked by bandits, sleeping rough and looking hungry. And, though Paul doesn't mention it here, you could include a picture of him in prison.

Eventually the pictures and models might become part of an exhibition in church, or a book, or part of a flower festival.

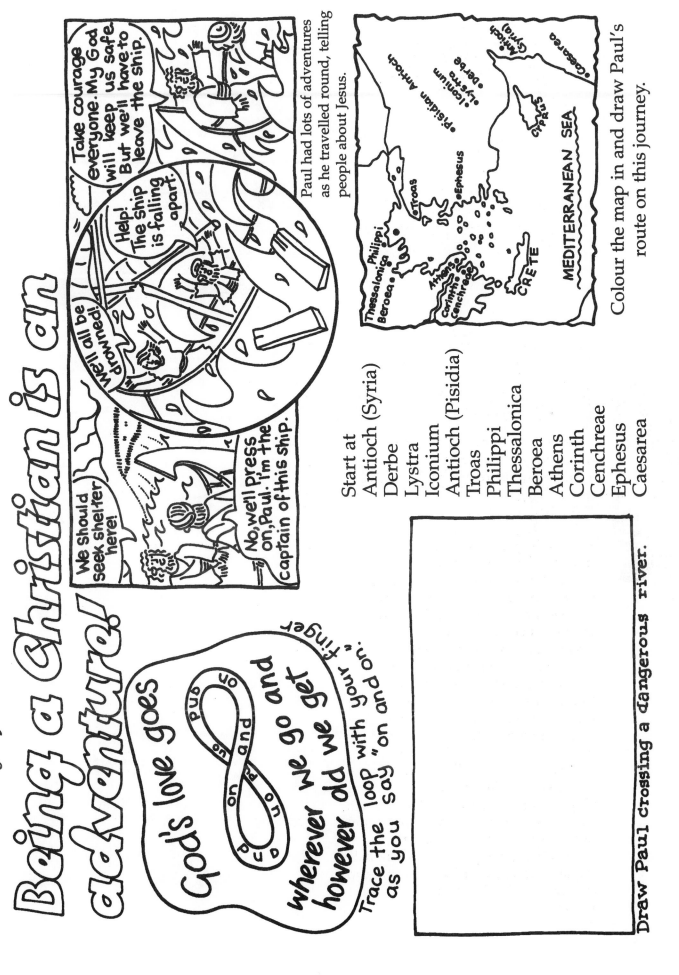

20th Sunday after Pentecost

YEAR 1

Thought for the day:
If we endure, we shall reign with him.

Readings
Psalm 51
Job 1
2 Timothy 2:1-19

Aim: For the children to learn abut the value of enduring and persevering.

Start with a guessing game, such as 'I spy', where we sometimes admit defeat, and give up. As you are playing, notice whether people give up easily, or keep pressing on, and mention this afterwards.

Tell the story of the first chapter of Job, using the carpet tiles method, and cut outs of Job, his family and all his herds of animals. As each disaster strikes, the appropriate cut out is taken away, until Job is left all on his own.

Talk together about how hard it is to stay cheerful when things keep going wrong, and how Job refused to let his sufferings turn him away from God.

Then help the children to make this model to help them remember.

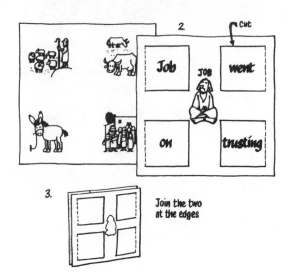

What about the bad times?

We do not always feel ☺.
We all have ☹ times as well.

Think of the ☹
you have had

Here's what to do about them.

1. If it happened because you were being selfish

2. If it happened because someone was nasty to you

3. If it couldn't be helped, but was still sad

Forgive them!

Colour this picture of fitness training.

Sometimes the bad times can...

Tell God you are sorry. Let him forgive you and help put things right.

Remember that it made God sad, too. He will help you cope with it, and bring good from it.

20th Sunday after Pentecost

YEAR 2

Thought for the day:
If we endure, we shall reign with him.

Readings
Psalm 51
Jeremiah 38:1-13
James 1:1-15

Aim: For the children to hear the story of Jeremiah, and understand about not giving up.

Start with a fitness session of running on the spot, jumping, skipping and sit ups. While everyone relaxes, have some quiet music, and talk about how hard it is sometimes to keep going on something we find difficult, but God will help us, often through our friends.

Tell the story of Jeremiah, using a large scale version of the model the children will be making.

Then help the children to make a model of Jeremiah being pulled out of the muddy well. You will need a large plastic pot (yoghurt type), some plastic from other bottles and pots to cut Jeremiah out of, some bits of material, string and scissors. Either make the sloshy mud yourselves by adding water to some earth from outside, or have this already made.

Paint outside stone colour

Mud inside

Thick cotton thread

Paper clips to weight

When things go wrong

Life is not always easy, is it? We all have bad times and sad times.

THINGS THAT GO WRONG

How does God help?

God can...

us Help brave. to be

us Help friends again. make

He us company will keep

us forgive. He help can to

Comfort will God us.

Can you unjumble these?

Look at the pictures. Which ones happen to you?

Draw a different one here if you like.

How can we work with God?

We can after another. another

give another and another.

21st Sunday after Pentecost

Help them to make this stand up model of looking into the distance at the same time as seeing the immediate present.

YEAR 1

Thought for the day:
In his own good time, God is drawing all things to perfect completion.

Readings
Psalms 23,24 or 78:1-24
Ezekiel 34:11-24
2 Peter 3

Aim: For the children to see how Ezekiel's prophecy came true in Jesus, and look forward to the second coming of Christ.

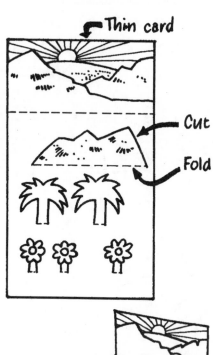

Begin with setting out a whole lot of things that measure time, and work out together their order, starting with the smallest time measurement. So your assortment might include a stopwatch, egg timer, watch or clock, and calendar or diary. Use a simple time line (showing us, Jesus, Ezekiel, Moses and Abraham) to make it clear what time Ezekiel was writing and who he was. Then have the passage read out by two good readers.

Ask the children if it reminds them of anything Jesus said or did. No matter if they don't make the connection on their own. Look at a picture of Jesus, the good shepherd, and read or tell the children about how in Jesus, Ezekiel's prophecy came true, some time after it was written.

Now remind the children that Jesus is going to return to us in glory some time – we don't know when, but we know it will happen because he said it would happen and he speaks the truth and always keeps to what he says. If they want to talk and ask questions about this, answer simply and honestly – including 'I don't know' if you don't.

21st Sunday after Pentecost

God is bringing it all together

When, when, when, when?

We know that one day... years will come again but we don't know when that will be.

A good bit of advice is to stay ready if it isn't missy oot fast! (then you know you'll be ready!)

to measure minutes
to measure months
to measure days
to measure years
to measure hours
to measure seconds

21st Sunday after Pentecost

YEAR 2

Thought for the day:
In his own good time, God is drawing
all things to perfect completion.

Readings
Psalms 23,24 or 78:1-24
Job 4:1 and 5:1-16
Hebrews 10:19-end

Aim: For the children to know that with God nothing is impossible, and we can put our hope in him.

Bring a vacuum cleaner in with you today.

Begin with that excellent eating game, where you throw a dice in turn and when you get six you run up to the front, put on thick gloves and a scarf, and start to eat a chocolate bar with a knife and fork. As soon as someone else throws a six they take over.

After the game, talk about how we were all living hopefully as the dice came round, hoping that we would get a six. We are going to look at a hope which won't make any of us disappointed, because we can all win.

Now ask someone to do a spot of vacuuming, but before they start, ask the children how they know the vacuum will clear up the mess. Their trust in it will be based on past experience. (Try the cleaner to check that it really does work.) It is our past experience of God that makes us know he is worth trusting, and can do the impossible in deadlock situations.

Take the children on a whistle stop tour of the wonders God performed (as in today's psalm) in Egypt, and share any more recent wonders that have happened in your own experience.

Learn to trust God

22nd Sunday after Pentecost

YEARS 1 AND 2

Thought for the day:
You cannot live with self and God both at the centre of your life; you will have to choose between them.

Readings
Psalms 42,43
Proverbs 14:31-15:17
James 4:13-5:11

Aim: For the children to understand the choice we have to make in the way we live.

In pairs play the 'Stone, paper, scissors' game, where each child makes a choice at the same time, and shows the appropriate hand sign. Stone wins over scissors (because it can break them), scissors wins over paper (because they can cut it), and paper wins over stone (because it can wrap around it).

Now have the James passage written as if it is a real letter, in a stamped addressed envelope, and explain how

James was writing to all the scattered Jewish Christians, and was very bothered about some unchristian behaviour. See if they can spot what this is. Use a translation such as the *International Children's Bible* where the shorter sentence structure makes it much easier to understand.

List all the things the children can remember, and then work out together how James is really wanting them to live. List these things next to the bad things in a different colour.

Talk together about how hard it is to choose to live God's way. For instance, we may know we should be honest, but when we want to stay out of trouble and get frightened of what will happen if someone finds out what we've done, we really want to tell lies. Explain how we can ask Jesus to give us the courage to choose the right way, and he will help us.

Now help the children to make this model to remind them each day. They can choose which centre to put into their life – God or self.

1. Roll out self-hardening clay.

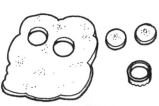

2. With a pastry cutter, cut out two 'plugs'.

3. Make and decorate a shape with a hole in the middle.

4. Write on one plug 'GOD' and on the other 'SELF'.

5. Keep the plugs next to the model. Each morning choose which plug to put in.

22nd Sunday after Pentecost

God or Self? You choose!

being kind

cheating

being mean

leaving someone out at playtime

helping at home

GOD/SELF

being grumpy

being friendly

giving time to people

being bossy

sharing

Colour the good things the same colour as GOD.
Colour the selfish things the same colour as SELF.

1. Draw a car or a wedding.
2. Make it sunny or raining.
3. Colour it or leave it as it is.

How do you know what is right and what is wrong?

You have just made three 'choices'. God has made us able to choose.

Listen to your:

Last Sunday after Pentecost

YEAR 1

Thought for the day:
Heaven is our home.

Readings
Psalm 89:1-18
Daniel 10:2-19
Revelation 1:1-18

Aim: For the children to learn about heaven.

Strangely enough, one of the only parts of the Christian faith nominal Christians tell their children is that people (and often animals) who have died are in heaven, living with Jesus. It is, after all, a comforting story. Yet in church this is the area least covered, I find. If we don't talk much of this area of faith, children will sooner or later think of heaven as a baby story which they have to grow out of. So let's go for it, and bring all those secret questions into the open.

Start by asking the children what they think happens when a person's body wears out and dies. Listen carefully to their answers, so as to address any worries or misunderstandings you hear hinted at. Talk to them about what heaven is like, homing in on the qualities, rather than on what it may or may not look like. What is important is that they begin to get a sense of a place which is happy, welcoming, loving and suitable for all ages! Make it clear that people do not turn into angels when they die, they won't have to hang around on clouds getting bored all day, and it isn't somewhere you could reach by spaceship. The only way in is by dying, after choosing good, rather than evil,

through your life. Read to them Daniel's vision of heaven, and point out how lovingly Daniel is treated.

Then let them express their own ideas of heaven in painting, drawing, creative writing or clay.

Heaven is our home

In heaven we will be very happy living with Jesus.

Heaven is our SPIRITUAL home. It is lovely and we can live there for ever.

Draw and colour what you think heaven is like.

Heaven

Here are some homes people live in. Which is which?

house
bungalow
houseboat
TENT
caravan
mud hut
flat
the street

This is OUR EARTHLY home.

What about after we die?
Where will we live then?

We won't need our when we get to heaven.

(We won't need our when we get to heaven.)

Last Sunday after Pentecost

YEAR 2

Thought for the day:
Heaven is our home.

Readings
Psalm 89:1-18
Ezekiel 11:14-21
Hebrews 13:1-21

Aim: For the children to enjoy behaving as citizens of the kingdom of heaven.

First try guessing what job people have from the mime they perform. Then explain that we are citizens – both of our own city, and of heaven. Jesus has opened the way for us. How should we not behave, as children? How should grown ups not behave?

Have a large sheet of paper with a journey drawn on it (as shown below), and some separate cards. Write the children's suggestions for both kinds of behaviour on the cards, in different coloured pens, and then play the game, taking turns to throw the dice. They will no doubt notice that we have only one counter, so although it's a journey we're on it isn't a race. Every time you throw the dice you pick a card. If it is right behaviour the counter is moved forward; if not it's moved backwards.

Then the children can make their own pocket version to take home.

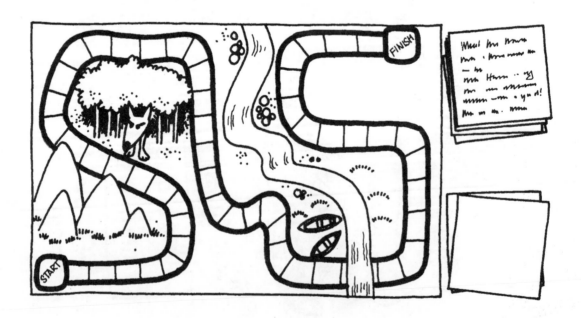

Last Sunday after Pentecost

ON THE WAY TO HEAVEN

Will there be room for me?

Has anyone come back from heaven?

I do bad things sometimes. Will God chuck me out?

Will my body be old and ill? Will I die in heaven when I am old and ill?

Jesus has. And some people have got close when they were very ill.

No, your spirit will be happy and free. You don't need your body in heaven.

Not if you are sorry and want to go. God forgives you, and loves you.

Yes. Jesus has promised there is that room.

WHAT IS HEAVEN LIKE?

```
W O N D E R F U L P
A K O M T N T O R E
B E T T E R V Q G A
Z J B L R I O Y D C
C K A H N H U S J E
D S E G A I N C X F
M H F E L P B A S U
G V O R P L P R H L
F I P M W C Q Y O D
D I F F E R E N T T
```

WONDERFUL HAPPY
PEACEFUL HOME
ETERNAL NOT SCARY
DIFFERENT LOVING
BETTER